G000134826

WALKING THE
WEST SUSSEX COAST
• A COMPANION GUIDE •

PHIL CHRISTIAN

Published in 2021
Copyright © 2021 Phil Christian

All rights reserved. Apart from any fair dealing for the purpose of private study, research, criticism or review, as permitted under the Copyright, Designs and Patents Act, 1988, no part of this publication may be reproduced, stored in a retrieval system, or transmitted in any form or by any means, electronic, electrical, chemical, mechanical, optical, photocopying, recording or otherwise, without the prior written permission of the copyright owner. Enquiries should be addressed to the Publishers.

Every attempt has been made by the author and publisher to secure the appropriate permissions for materials reproduced in this book. If there has been any oversight we will be happy to rectify the situation in future editions following a written submission made to the Publishers.

A CIP catalogue record for this book is available from the British Library.

ISBN: 978 0 85710 130 3

PiXZ Books
Halsgrove House, Ryelands Business Park,
Bagley Road, Wellington,
Somerset TA21 9PZ
Tel: 01823 653777
Fax: 01823 216796
email: sales@halsgrove.com

An imprint of Halstar Ltd, part of the Halsgrove group of companies.
Information on all Halsgrove titles is available at: www.halsgrove.com

Printed and bound in India by Parksons Graphics

Front cover: Bognor beach is shingle with sand when the tide is out.
Contents: View across Bosham Channel to Holy Trinity church.

CONTENTS

MAP OF COASTLINE AND WALK LOCATIONS

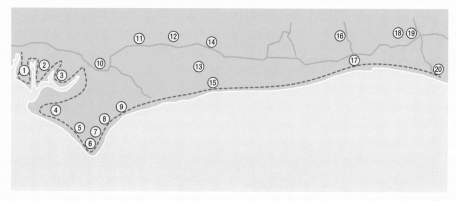

WALK	LOCATION	DISTANCE	ATTRACTION
1	Thorney Island	8.00mi 12.9km	Chichester Harbour and Pilsey Island.
2	Chidham	5.50mi 8.90km	Chichester Harbour and Cobnor Point.
3	Bosham	3.25mi 5.00km	Bosham Channel views and King Canute.
4	East & West Wittering & West Itchenor	9.00mi 14.5km	West Wittering's sandy beach, East Head and The Spit.
5	Medmerry RSPB Nature Reserve	3.00mi 4.80km	Medmerry new RSPB Nature Reserve.
6	Selsey	4.00mi 6.40km	Lifeboat Station and Medmerry Windmill.
7	Church Norton	5.00mi 8.00km	St Peters Church and St Wilfrid's Chapel.
8	Pagham (Selsey)	2.00mi 3.20km	RSPB Nature Reserve.
9	Pagham (Pagham)	3.75mi 6.00km	Pagham Harbour Nature Reserve.
10	Chichester	6.00mi 9.70km	Chichester Cathedral and city.
11a	Boxgrove	2.5mi 4.0km	Boxgrove Priory.
11b	Halnaker	1.75mi 2.8km	Halnaker Windmill.
12	Slindon	5.00mi 8.00km	Nore Folly and 'crick'.
13	Tortington	4.25mi 6.80km	'Beakhead Monsters' and River Arun.
14	Arundel	4.75mi 7.60km	Arundel Castle, Hiorne Tower and River Arun.
15	Climping	4.25mi 6.80km	Climping sand dunes and Littlehampton Harbour.
16	Bramber	7.00mi 11.3km	Bramber Castle ruins and River Adur.
17	Lancing & Shoreham	10.0mi 16.1km	Lancing College, views and River Adur.
18	Poynings	3.25mi 5.20km	Devil's Dyke.
19	Pyecombe	4.00mi 6.40km	Jack & Jill windmills and Clayton rail tunnel.
20	Brighton City Centre	4.00mi 6.40km	Two Piers, i360 and Royal Pavilion.

INTRODUCTION

West Sussex is my home county and I live in Selsey which lies at the southernmost point of the Manhood Peninsula almost cut off from mainland Sussex by the sea. The West Sussex coast is about 50 miles (80 km) long and although it can't boast of dramatic scenery like cliffs and bays, or contain colonies of seals basking on rocks or puffins on cliffs, it still has plenty to offer if you know where to look. To the south of the West Sussex coast is the English Channel, most of the beaches are pebbles and, of course it is officially the sunniest place in the UK according to Meteorological Office records; over the last twenty-nine years it has enjoyed an average of 1902 hours of sunshine a year. The coastline is laced with promenades and piers, numerous attractions and plenty of places to eat and drink. The West Sussex coast starts at Thorney Island and technically finishes at Portslade but for the purpose of this book I have extended it by a few miles to include Brighton which is arguably the most popular and well-known location in this area.

The westernmost part of this coast between Thorney Island and West Wittering is located around the various channels of Chichester Harbour which is a 3733-hectare Site of Special Scientific Interest (SSSI). Here are the villages of Bosham which is famous for the legend of King Canute (who commanded the waves to go back as he demonstrated the limits of his king's powers to his courtiers) and West Wittering which is famous for its large sandy beach. As already mentioned, Selsey sits at the end of the Manhood Peninsula which juts out into the sea with Selsey Bill at the furthest point. Pagham Harbour, although one harbour, is essentially divided into two parts: near to Selsey there is the RSPB area which is dedicated to birdwatching with a new Ferry Hide which overlooks Ferry Pool and there is a Visitors' Centre; the other area is in Pagham and although still dedicated to birdlife it is more open with fewer facilities but better suited for longer walks.

Thornham Marina, Thorney Island.

Famous pure white sands at West Wittering beach.

Visitors' Centre known as the Salthouse at
Pagham Harbour Nature Reserve.

The Waterside pub at Shoreham-by-Sea.

After Pagham you reach Bognor Regis and from now the coastline is much more built up with residential and industrial buildings and Bognor Regis, Littlehampton, Worthing and other smaller towns and villages dominate the coastline. I have written about these places and included photos but there are no walks. Instead, there are walks that are a short distance inland at places like Boxgrove, Slindon, Tortington and Arundel which I am sure you will prefer.

Lancing and Shoreham-by-Sea are both located beneath the South Downs National Park. Lancing College, which is a local landmark, has a predominantly nineteenth-century chapel that is the largest school chapel in the world. Shoreham-by-Sea is bordered by the River Adur which further upstream passes beside the ruins of Bramber Castle; Shoreham Airport is the oldest licenced airfield in the UK and was opened in 1911.

The final stage of this coastline goes between Shoreham-by-Sea and Brighton via Southwick and Portslade. Southwick is a small town and Portslade is officially where West Sussex ends but we are going to continue for a few more miles to include Hove and Brighton. In 1997, as part of a local government reform, the borough of Hove merged with Brighton to form the Borough of Brighton and Hove and this authority was then granted city status in 2000. I have included two walks just inland from Brighton to visit Devil's Dyke, the locally famous Jack and Jill windmills and the architecturally ornate Clayton train tunnel.

All the main coastal locations are featured in the book with relevant information and photos to help bring this coastline to life. All the walks have been carefully chosen to give maximum interest and, in most cases, to show their relationship to this coastline. Detailed maps are not provided in the book, however. Readers are recommended to refer to the relevant OS maps for the Sussex Coast.

CHAPTER 1
THORNEY ISLAND

Welcome. We begin our West Sussex coastal journey around the lovely Thorney Island. The island is technically a peninsula that juts out into Chichester Harbour but it is separated from the mainland by a channel called the Great Deep which you have to cross twice when walking around this island. To the east of Thorney Island is Chidham which is clearly visible and it is Chidham that you will be visiting and walking in Chapter 2. To the west is Hayling Island in South Hampshire and you can even see the top of the Spinnaker Tower in Portsmouth.

Thornham Point was at the tip of a small peninsula until 1870 but today two sea walls enclose 186 acres of reclaimed land known as Eames Farm which join Thorney Island to the mainland. The island is an ideal wildlife haven particularly in the Great and Little Deeps, the two tidal channels that run across it; Eames Farm became part of a habitat creation scheme in 1996. The tide flows in and out through a gap in the sea wall and the saltmarsh areas contain plants that are capable of surviving in salt water, such as sea purslane and glasswort.

View across Prinsted Channel towards Chidham.

Thornham Marina.

Waders and wildfowl come to the harbour in the winter to feed on the intertidal mud. Greenshank have been monitored here for over fifteen years and other notable species to look out for include wigeon, black-tailed godwit and red-breasted mergansers in the Deeps and the more elusive pintail or great northern diver in the Channel. The island is also home to the rare large gold case-bearer moth and this is one of the strongest colonies in the UK. The larvae feed on Dyers greenweed in the spring then become moths during July and August. You can also spot dark-bellied brent geese and golden plover in the winter and in the summer, there are skylarks singing and sedge, reed and Cetti's warblers chattering in the reedbeds; an osprey may pass through in spring or early autumn.

Thorney Island is best known for its association with the British military. On the 25th September 1933 a Hawker Fury biplane crashed on Thorney Island, killing the pilot and during the accident investigation officials from the Air Ministry realised that this would be the ideal place for an airbase. In 1938 an RAF airbase was built, the runways being metalled in 1942. The men from the Air

Ministry were proved right in their judgement as Thorney Island was well used by the RAF during WWII. From here bombing raids on German ports and shipping, reconnaissance flights and coastal patrol operations all took place.

In common with many RAF Coastal Command airfields a great variety of squadrons and aircraft were stationed here during the war. Among the aircraft based here was the Avro Anson; this was a British twin-engine, multi-role aircraft built by Avro in large numbers. They served a variety of roles for the RAF, Royal Canadian Air Force and other air forces before, during and after WWII.

Post war between 1965-69 the airfield was used as an instructional unit, training aircrew and navigators on Varsity, Argosy and Beverley aircraft and in 1968 it was responsible for the introduction of the first C130 Hercules. The RAF left the island in 1976. In 1984 the base was renamed as Baker Barracks and was to house a Royal Artillery unit, the 26th Field Regiment Royal Artillery armed with the FH70 – a towed howitzer used by several nations. Later the 26th Regiment was replaced by the 47th Regiment Royal Artillery armed with the Starstreak High Velocity Missile – a British short-range man-portable air defence system. In 2008 the 12th Regiment Royal Artillery moved in upon their return from Germany and 47 Regiment subsequently relocated to Larkhill in Wiltshire as part of the restructuring of the British Army 2020 programme and and remain there today.

In 2009 the airfield was used as a test track for a British-built steam car that was trying to smash the longest standing land speed record. The British Steam Car Challenge team included test driver Don Wales who is the nephew of the late Donald Campbell and the grandson of Sir Malcolm Campbell.

The church of St Nicholas is an Anglican parish church near the end of Thorney Island. It is dedicated to St Nicholas, the patron saint especially of sailors and it served a harbour community of farmers and seafarers. The original building dates from c1100, constructed probably on the orders of Bishop Warlewast – a great church builder. Within the church grounds is a Commonwealth War Graves Commission cemetery dedicated to 51 Allied servicemen and 21 German airmen of WWII.

Waterside path.

Typical waterside path looking across Prinsted Channel.

The Great Deep.

Approaching East Gate security check.

Church of St. Nicholas.

There are also 46 graves and memorials to servicemen and women who were based on Thorney Island who died in the service of their nation. They are buried in regimented rows facing Chichester Harbour.

At the southernmost tip of the island is Longmere Point and Pilsey Island. Longmere Point is an 18-hectare RSPB reserve and from here you can see East Head at West Wittering (Walk 4) and on a clear day you can glimpse the Isle of Wight. Pilsey Island is a small island in Chichester Harbour, just off the south-eastern tip of Thorney Island and in recent years it has become joined to Thorney by accumulating sand. The island is best known for bird watchers as the small reserve comprises a wide range of coastal habitats: intertidal sandflats and mudflats, dunes, bare and vegetated shingle and saltmarsh. There is a variety of unusual plants, spiders and insects that thrive on the reserve and the area of Pilsey Sand is an important pre-roost and roost site for passage and wintering waders in the area.

In the summer oystercatchers and ringed plovers breed in the shingle ridges at Pilsey Island and skylarks breed in the dunes; terns have bred here in the past. The highlight for most people would be to spot a harbour seal and although I have done this walk three times now, I have never seen one so it looks like I've got to go back for a fourth time. They are regularly spotted across the Solent and up to thirty harbour seals and six grey seals have been seen in Chichester Harbour at any one time. This group is the only known resident population (rookery) in the eastern English Channel and they can occasionally be seen on the mudflats where they rest sometimes in a "banana" shape with their tails and heads raised up.

Now that you have read this chapter about Thorney Island, I hope you will do Walk 1 and then you can experience for yourself what this magical island has to offer. I will see you in Chapter 2 to continue our coastal walk around Chidham.

Longmere Point.

Pilsey Island.

View towards Marker Point - look for seals in this area.

Raised bank with Emsworth ahead and army canoeists.

SUGGESTED WALK

WALK 1. Thorney Island (8 miles 12.9 km)

Parking. There is a car park at the end of Prinsted Lane by a Sea Scout Group building. (Post code PO10 8HS.) This is a lovely walk around the perimeter of Thorney Island with views all around. The walk is completely level and there are no stiles, making it a fairly easy walk as long as you give yourself enough time. The island is surrounded by Chichester Harbour so you are totally exposed to the weather. Check the weather forecast to make sure there is no rain forecast or wind as you will be buffeted the whole way. Try to pick a sunny day as this will result in you getting the best views and some lovely photographs but remember your cap, especially if you are thin on top like I am. There is nowhere to buy refreshments on this walk so take a drink and something to eat; there are numerous well-placed viewing benches throughout the walk where you can have a rest and enjoy the views whilst having your lunch. I recommend that you take a map of Chichester Harbour with you. As you do Walks 1 to 4 you can see points you recognise across the channels and this will help you understand the geography of the harbour. For example, Thorney Island Sailing Club is visible from Chidham (Walk 2) and Itchenor (Walk 4).

1. From the car park go ahead at a 3-way footpath sign, pass between a wooden barrier and continue ahead with Chichester Harbour (Prinsted Channel) on the left following the slightly raised path heading towards the boats at Thornham Marina. Go through the marina, crossing two wooden bridges and continue ahead soon crossing a more substantial wooden bridge. When the path turns right by a small bench you have reached Prinsted Point and in a further 35 yards you go left at a signpost and continue through a squeeze stile.

2. At a Ministry of Defence (MoD) security fence across the Great Deep (East Gate) you have to request access to continue via an intercom and you may be asked a few basic security questions. (It is also possible that you just hear a click and the operator will have opened the gate remotely for you – just push the gate and continue.) From here onwards, until you leave on the other side, you must keep to the perimeter path and follow the yellow marker posts and footpath signs as all the inner area is private MoD land that is patrolled by guard dogs.

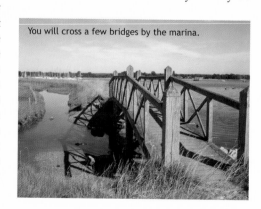

You will cross a few bridges by the marina.

Follow the path beside Thorney Channel with Chidham in view to your left and when the path juts out to the left and becomes slightly gravelled you have reached Stanbury Point. Just continue until you reach St Nicholas's church where you side-step to the right, up three concrete steps, and continue along the left edge of the church grounds; you can visit the church if it is open and the war graves which are to the right of the church.

Just past the church you reach Thorney Island Sailing Club (TISC). This is a very useful reference point for the next few walks as you will be able to see it from Chidham (Walk 2) and Itchenor (Walk 4) and this will help you understand the geographic layout of Chichester Harbour. Get an image of this building in your mind and look out for it on future walks.)

Immediately beyond the church you turn right up an access drive as directed by a footpath sign and in 15 yards go left at another footpath sign along an access road signed as High Water Footpath. At the end of the small parking area continue ahead along an enclosed path passing the Thorney Island Watersports Centre on the left. The path soon arrives back at the water's edge at Thorney Channel where you turn right and continue as before. Soon the path runs parallel with a tarmac road on your right and then continues on an enclosed path between trees, bushes and hawthorns, from which it is possible the island gets its name as the island is covered in them. At the end of the enclosed area, by a barrier and MoD signs, you have reached Longmere Point by Pilsey Island on the left which you can explore and there is an information board about the area.

Thornham Marina.

St Nicholas church.

Regimented rows of war graves looking out over Chichester Harbour.

Thorney Island Sailing Club – visible from Walks 2 and 4.

3. From the barrier and MoD signs you continue ahead on a narrow and slightly overgrown path heading towards a wooden bird hide, from which you get a good view across Pilsey Island, Hayling Island and the Spinnaker Tower at Portsmouth. Also, keep a look out for harbour seals which have been spotted here; you will have to be lucky as I have done this walk three times and never seen one. Continue past the bird hide and follow the grassy path as it gradually curves to the right and then back to the left heading towards Marker Point which you can see in the distance; Marker Point is then reached just after going around / through a wooden gate and arriving at a 2-way footpath sign by a viewing bench.

4. Continue and just follow the winding perimeter path with Emsworth Channel on the left and Hayling Island in view on the other side of the channel. Just keep going passing through a wooden gate and then a little further on a swing gate before eventually reaching the MoD security fence (West Gate) where you leave the island using the intercom to register that you are leaving.

Pilsey Island bird hide.

5. On the other side of the gate pass through a wooden squeeze point and go ahead along a raised bank with Emsworth in view ahead. At the end of the raised bank you reach a row of white waterfront properties. At a 3-way footpath sign next to the properties go right along a grassy path which is soon enclosed between trees and bushes.

Go through a metal swing gate, ahead across a farm area and continue along an access drive to reach a road via a swing gate. Cross the road and go ahead along Thornham Lane opposite. Follow the lane until you turn left along Prinsted Lane which takes you back to the start.

Leave the island along a raised bank.

High security Ministry of Defence exit from Thorney Island.

CHAPTER 2
CHIDHAM

The second part of our journey takes us to the lovely, but smaller than Thorney Island, coastal village of Chidham. Still part of Chichester Harbour it has the Thorney Channel to the west and Bosham Channel to the east. Thorney Island, Bosham and Itchenor can all easily be seen from Chidham and at one point in our walk we can get some particularly nice photographs across the Bosham Channel of the Holy Trinity church in Bosham where it is believed that King Canute's daughter is buried.

PLEASE NOTE: – an area of the beach close to Cobnor Point near the very south tip of Chidham floods at high tide and is impassable; there is no alternative route. You need to check the times of the high tides to avoid getting blocked. You will reach Cobnor Point anywhere from about 60 to 90 minutes after starting your walk. For checking for high tides, I use *tidetimes.co.uk* and search for Chichester Harbour. Enter the date you are thinking of visiting and it will give you the time and heights of the tides.

View across Bosham Channel to Holy Trinity church where it is believed King Canute's daughter is buried.

Like Thorney Island Chidham is a Site of Special Scientific Interest and is a wetland of international importance, a Special Protection Area for wild birds and a Special Area of Conservation. The harbour is important for wintering wildfowl and waders of which five species reach numbers which are internationally important.

Beach near Cobnor Point that floods every high tide.

Mirror image of a little egret.

Black headed gull.

The name of Chidham is derived from the Old English words ceod (meaning bag or pouch) and ham (meaning settlement) and refers to the shape of the peninsula on which it is situated. During a recent excavation Chidham has revealed that man made use of Chidham more than 4000 years ago. The flint scrapers found on a site on the western shore of the peninsula, suggest that spear shafts or kiddles (fish traps) and primitive salterns (a method for making salt) were being made here. It is thought that the Saxon Saint Cuthman may have been born in Chidham c681. The church of St Mary's dates from the thirteenth century and may have had a wooden predecessor.

The peninsula is not mentioned in the Domesday book because it formed part of the Manor or Chapelry of Bosham, rich in farming land and then belonging to the Bishop of Exeter. The men of Chidham seem to have been farmers rather than fisherman possibly due to the good quality of the soil and during the walk you will notice that most of the inner part of Chidham is still used for growing various

One of many places to sit and enjoy the views.

Wooden perimeter bridge with typical view.

This whole area is popular for sailing.

crops. In 1812 an embankment was constructed from Chidham to Bosham, using an old quay. Writing about Bosham in the 1860s Charles Longcroft described how the newly enclosed land was ploughed and planted with corn. 'But one November, there came a raging tide and gale wind, from the southwest and away went the embankment.' In 1825 the sea returned covering the farmland and flooding new buildings, one of the buildings is said to have been a mansion at Cutmill, whose stone was later used to build Cutmill Cottage.

Today parts of the Chidham peninsula are at risk from tidal flooding as you will see whilst doing your walk. With global warming, rising sea levels and more powerful and regular storms flooding is becoming more of a problem in the Chichester Harbour area as well as parts of Selsey and Pagham.

During WWII bombs were recorded as falling within the parish of Chidham. On the night of 8 October 1940, the vicarage, now the Old Rectory, was damaged by an incendiary and a torpedo bomber, carrying a crew of four, crashed close to the church. The fire in the vicarage was quickly extinguished by the local volunteer fire service but the aeroplane proved a greater hazard. On the night of 25-26 April 1941, during a raid on Portsmouth, seven high explosive bombs fell near Manor Farm.

As stated on an information board near Cobnor Point the intertidal areas of Chichester Harbour are special because they are important wildlife habitats and are highly protected under UK and European law. The saltmarsh is a protected habitat and this area is important for attracting wading birds and as a source for their food. Plants that grow here can survive in salt water and will thrive in different places depending on the tide. For example, sea beet can tolerate sea spray but glasswort and sea purslane are covered daily by the tide. There is a good network of footpaths to enable enjoyable walks which give access to the shore and the intertidal mudflats of Chichester Harbour where you need to look out for bird life, insects, moths, butterflies etc.

Now let's do Walk 2 around the perimeter of Chidham, admiring the views of Chichester Harbour and looking out for the birdlife before I see you in Chapter 3 when we visit Bosham and the burial location of King Canute's daughter.

Relax and enjoy the views from Cobnor Point to Thorney Island and Itchenor.

Windswept trees by the beach near Cobnor Point.

SUGGESTED WALK

WALK 2. Chidham (5.5 miles 8.9 km)

Parking. Roadside parking in the area by the Old House at Home pub. (Post code PO18 8SU.) Once again, like Thorney Island, this is a lovely walk around the perimeter of Chidham with views all around. Throughout the 5.5 miles of this walk there are so many good views and varied birdlife and butterflies to look out for. The walk is completely level and there are no stiles making it a very easy walk. PLEASE REMEMBER that there is a section of beach near Cobnor Point that floods every high tide and is impassable; there is no alternative route. Chidham is also surrounded by Chichester Harbour so once again you are exposed to the weather; try to pick a sunny day as this will result in you getting the best views and some lovely photographs across to Thorney Island, Bosham and Itchenor, all places you will visit on other walks. I purposely started the walk by the Old House at Home as it is a nice pub that I have used each time I walk here and it is ideal for a drink at the start or end of your walk; or both. During the walk there are conveniently placed viewing benches, especially the well-sited one at Cobnor Point which has great views.

1. With your back to the pub, go right down Cot Lane, not signed and follow it around to the left. Pass St Mary's church on the left and the Old Rectory opposite and continue, soon following the lane as it turns sharp right. At the end you reach a junction with Steels Lane and Chidham Lane and you continue ahead, to the left of a house, as directed by the footpath sign that is next to the Chidham Lane road sign.

Typical perimeter path.

Go along the narrow path to the left of some large greenhouses and at the end go right and follow a right-hand field edge out to a lane. Go left along the lane and in 15 yards go right at a 3-way footpath sign along Harbour Way; follow this Pedestrian Only access staying strictly on the access road. At a grass roundabout go ahead on an enclosed path as directed by a 2-way footpath sign. Soon you arrive

Pools beside perimeter path - popular for birdlife.

beside the Bosham Channel with lovely views of the Holy Trinity church at Bosham Quay (Walk 3) clearly in view directly across Bosham Channel.

2. Turn right to go around the edge of the channel and in a few yards go up seven steps to a footpath sign and continue along the raised bank. Follow this bank, keeping a look out for varied birdlife, passing a well-placed small viewing bench and at a 3-way footpath sign go sharp left back to the channel's edge. Go right and continue to reach the boat-shaped Cobnor Activities Centre. A few

yards before it, go right down a concrete slope and go right at a 2-way footpath sign. Follow the path around the back of the Activities Centre and at an access road go right for 5 yards then go left at a footpath sign immediately crossing a sleeper bridge. Follow an enclosed path, passing footpath signs and boats to end up back at the channel on the other side of the Activities Centre.

Old House at Home pub.

Continue around the perimeter soon crossing two wooden bridges fairly close together to reach a solitary viewing bench at Cobnor Point. From this area you have views towards Thorney Island (Walk 1) and Itchenor (Walk 4) and it is well worth stopping here to fully appreciate the views and to fully understand your location within Chichester Harbour.

St Mary's church.

3. Continue along the perimeter path and soon, at a 2-way signpost, go left down wooden steps on to the beach. NOTE - this beach is the area that floods at high tide. Continue along the beach passing windswept trees, dead trees and Cobnor Bird Hide; this is a fascinating stretch of beach and makes for some interesting photos. As you go along the beach there are also good views across to the Thorney Island Sailing Club, that I said to remember when you did Walk 1.

View back up Bosham Channel.

View across Thorney Channel to Thorney Island Sailing Club.

Steps down to beach that floods.

Beach that floods at high tide.

After a few hundred yards, when the beach starts to curve around to the right, go up some basic wooden steps to an information board. Continue on the raised bank and just follow the grassy path with dips on either side and New Barn away to the right. As you go along this path look out for butterflies especially the marbled white; I did this walk in early July and there were hundreds of them. There are also many areas along this path that have large stones stacked up as part of the local sea defences.

Just follow this raised path to eventually arrive back at the water's edge by a wooden fence. Continue clockwise around the perimeter and soon you reach a 3-way footpath sign where you turn sharply right, back on yourself, down six steps. Follow the right field edge then go left and ahead across the centre of two fields. (This area, all the way back to the pub, can be full of crops at the right time of year.) Cross a plank bridge and continue ahead on the clear path to reach Cot Lane. Turn right along the lane back to the Old House at Home for well-deserved refreshments.

Cobnor Bird Hide.

CHAPTER 3
BOSHAM

View of Bosham from Shore Road.

Stage three of our journey takes us to the lovely but small coastal village of Bosham (pronounced "Bozzum") which is located on one of the smaller arms of Chichester Harbour on the Bosham Channel. Although Bosham has had an important part in history over the centuries it is probably fair to say that it is best known for two particular stories.

Firstly, legend has it that it was here that the Danish King Canute (also Cnut) sat on a chair whilst surrounded by his courtiers and commanded the waves to go back. When they did not, he got his feet wet showing that even the great Canute was mortal.

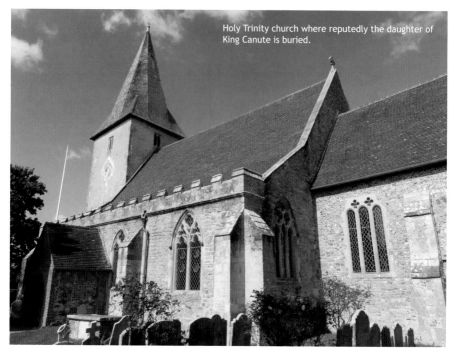

Holy Trinity church where reputedly the daughter of King Canute is buried.

Secondly, there is a strong belief that Canute's beloved eight-year-old daughter, who drowned in a millstream that runs through the village, is buried in the church of the Holy Trinity in a Saxon coffin at the base of the chancel steps. Although there is no proof of this, in 1865 a coffin containing a child's skeleton was discovered and this is thought to be Canute's daughter. The memorial is on public display.

The inscription on Canute's daughter's memorial reads: -

Memorial to Canute's daughter.

TO THE GLORY OF GOD
AND IN MEMORY OF
A DAUGHTER OF KING CANUTE
WHO DIED EARLY IN THE
11TH CENTURY
AGED ABOUT 8 YEARS
WHOSE REMAINS LIE ENCLOSED IN A
STONE COFFIN BENEATH THIS SPOT

PLACED BY THE CHILDREN OF
THE PARISH AUGUST 1906

Bosham Quay.

Inhabited by the Romans, Bosham was considered the sixth most important town in Sussex in the eighth century and it is close to the famous Roman Palace in Fishbourne. There have been a number of important Roman buildings found in the north of Bosham including a possible temple, a small theatre and a mosaic. In 1064 Harold II set forth from Bosham to negotiate with William of Normandy, a voyage that led to William the Conqueror's return in 1066. Bosham features in the Bayeaux Tapestry. Harold went to mass at Bosham (as depicted on the tapestry) before leaving to meet with William. At this meeting Harold told William that he would be claiming the throne of England for himself. William did not take kindly to this and as a consequence the battle of Hastings was fought in 1066. The tapestry shows Harold having a feast in the manor house followed by a blessing service in the church, before setting out in his long boat for Normandy.

The Bosham Head, part of the largest Roman statue from Britain was found nearby. It is a large 375-pound (170Kg) piece of sculpted stone discovered in Bosham around 1800. Later it resided for some time in the garden of the Bishop of Chichester's palace before being put on display at Chichester Museum where it remains. In 2013, Dr Miles Russell and Harry Manley of Bournemouth University

Bosham Head at the Novium Museum, Chichester.

used 3D laser scans and were able to conclude that enough of the sculpture had survived to suggest that the head was of Emperor Trajan and was possibly erected by Hadrian at the mouth of Chichester Harbour. A legionary helmet was found in Bosham Harbour which is now in the Lewes Museum; it is of late Claudian date, the time of the invasion. There is a tradition saying that Emperor Vespasian had a residence in Bosham although there is no proof of this. There are also said to be the remains of a building thought to be a villa belonging to Vespasian at the Stone Wall in the parish. Pottery and tile fragments from both Roman and early British periods have been found here confirming pre-Anglo-Saxon activity.

Most of Bosham's history in the Early Middle Ages is ecclesiastical (relating to the Christian church or its clergy). Bosham is mentioned by Bede in his book *The Ecclesiastical History of the English Nation*, when he speaks of Wilfrid's visit here in 681 when he encountered Dicul, an Irish monk, and five disciples in a small monastery. Bosham is one of only five places that appear on a map attached to the Anglo-Saxon Chronicle from around this time.

Holy Trinity church, believed to be the resting place of King Canute's daughter.

Holy Trinity church.

The millstream that runs through Bosham.

In 850, the original village church was built possibly on the site of a Roman building and this was replaced with the Holy Trinity church that is still there today. There is a legend that around the time of King Canute Bosham church was plundered by Danish pirates, who stole the tenor bell. As the pirate ship sailed away, the remaining bells were rung and when the tenor bell miraculously joined in it destroyed the ship. The bell is still said to ring beneath the waters whenever the other bells are rung.

For centuries Bosham was a fishing village that was famous for its oysters. For a small village Bosham is so popular that it can become very busy with walkers, cyclists, birdwatchers, artists, photographers, history lovers and visitors; it is very popular with sailors as it is also a centre for sailing. There are a couple of pubs with the Anchor Bleu overlooking the waterfront.

BE WARNED – at low tide it is possible to park your car in Bosham by the water's edge but as the tide comes in your car will be submerged. There is a pay-and-display car park in Bosham Lane if you just want to visit Bosham.

Now join me for Walk 3 around Bosham. I will then see you in Chapter 4 when we will continue around the Witterings and West Itchenor where you get to walk along the popular sandy beach of West Wittering.

The area is very popular for sailing.

At high tide the sea floods the road up to the raised wall.

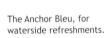

The Anchor Bleu, for waterside refreshments.

SUGGESTED WALK

WALK 3. Bosham (3.25 miles 5 km)

Parking. There is roadside parking at the end of Fairfield Road by the church of Our Lady of the Assumption. (Post code PO18 8JH.) Bosham is a lovely little village but this fairly short walk is crammed with so much else to see. The walk is completely level and there are no stiles to contend with. There are numerous places for refreshments including the Berkeley Arms at the very start and the Anchor Bleu pub by the water's edge. When you are at the water's edge remember it is tidal. If you look at the local shops and houses by the Anchor Bleu you will see how they have adapted flood defences across their doorways which will give you an idea of how high the sea can get at extremes.

View across Bosham Channel towards Chidham.

1. From the end of Fairfield Road by the church of Our Lady of the Assumption, go left along the main road using the right-hand pavement (the Berkeley Arms pub is a few yards to the right if you would like refreshments at the start). Turn right along Critchfield Road and follow it around to the left where it filters into Westbrook Field by a wide gate and a footpath sign. Go along this road, passing a 4-way footpath sign on the right and continue to reach the Bosham Channel.

Refreshments at the Berkeley Arms?

Go left beside the channel on the gravel path heading towards Bosham Quay; Chidham is on the other side of the channel. Soon you reach a boat launching area and a stone wall ahead, you now have to make a decision. If the tide is out you can continue ahead along the beach, passing Quay Meadow, the Quay Masters Office and the Anchor Bleu to reach Bosham Lane at section 2; this is the scenic route. However, if the tide is in you need to go left as I will now describe. Go left up the access road, pass a wide metal gate and continue to reach a road by a 3-way footpath sign.

Bosham Quay.

Go right along Moreton Road, not signed, and at its end go right down Bosham Lane using the left-hand pavement. Follow the road to its end, passing an Arts and Crafts Centre on the right to reach Bosham Quay.

2. From the Quay go back up Bosham Lane for 5 yards, and then go left along a minor road passing a café and the Anchor Bleu pub; as you go along this side road look at the doorways to

View across Bosham Channel.

the buildings and how the owners have fashioned flood defences to protect their doorways against the sea in extreme conditions. Continue for a few more yards to reach the church of the Holy Trinity, the burial location of King Canute's daughter.

Leave the church and turn right down the road to reach Quay Meadow. On the right of the green is a war memorial, commemorating both World Wars and if you look at the names you can see that some families from this small village lost more than one son. From here go left and walk back along the channel's edge to arrive back at Bosham Lane.

Now continue ahead beside the channel using the upper path behind the wall if the tide is in. Follow the path around to the right of the channel passing a 3-way footpath sign to reach a converted house with a "National School 1834" sign on it and in another 15 yards you reach a road junction. (The walk goes left here but you can do a short detour and go right to follow Shore Road for a lovely view back across to Old Bosham and the church; this is particularly good on a sunny day.)

3. At the junction, go left, along Stumps Lane, not signed, and follow it to reach Taylors Lane, not signed, at the end. Now taking care as there is no pavement for 20 yards, go left along the lane. Follow the lane for about 200 yards then go left along Leander Road. In a few yards keep to the left, immediately passing Astra Close and Shamrock Close on the left. Continue ahead and take the second road on the right, Fairfield Road (not Fairfield Close), back to the start.

Quay Meadow.

View back of Bosham from Shore Road.

CHAPTER 4

WEST ITCHENOR, WEST WITTERING & EAST WITTERING

The fourth stage of our journey, with the exception of a short distance on Walk 8 at Apuldram, is the final part of our journey around Chichester Harbour. East and West Wittering takes us along beach routes whilst West Itchenor, which is a popular location for yachting, completes the main part of Chichester Harbour.

West Itchenor boatyard.

EAST WITTERING

East Wittering is a coastal village on the Manhood Peninsula between West Wittering to the west and Bracklesham to the east. The village is slightly bigger than its neighbour Bracklesham but they both share the seafront of Bracklesham Bay. The popular beaches that extend into West Wittering get very busy in the summer but in the winter these beaches are subjected to strong winds and crashing waves. The beaches are pebbles at the top with the sandy areas exposed when the tide is out; if you want the sandy areas be prepared to move when the sea comes back in. Because of the boom in tourism and the ease with which people can reach East Wittering from London, East Wittering has expanded greatly and the village has spread so far along the seafront that part of the village lies within the parish of West Wittering. For many centuries the sea has pounded East Wittering resulting in the loss of many hundreds of acres of land, lost to the sea forever.

There has been a settlement at East Wittering for over a thousand years. The Witterings were included in a grant of land to Bishop Wilfred in the late seventh century and the area is mentioned in the Domesday Book as part of the Hundred of Westringes (later Manhood). For centuries the manor of East Wittering was in the hands of the Wystryng family, who took their name from the place.

East Wittering is sometimes mentioned as one of the Thankful Villages. It is one of only 32 villages in England and Wales and the only one in West Sussex, that suffered no casualties during the First World War. In May 1944 East Wittering became the landing beach for the 3rd Canadian Infantry Division during a dummy run for D-Day, code named Operation Fabius. Since then it has become a quiet area popular with surfers. Nikolaus Pevsner (1902-1983 architectural historian best known for his 46-volume series of county-by-county guides – The Buildings of England 1951-74) described East Wittering as 'a jumble of bungalows and chalets near the beach in an untidy half grown up state'.

St Anne's Anglican church was designed by Harry Sherwood who was surveyor of the fabric of Chichester Cathedral. The foundation stone was laid on 6 June 1958 and the Bishop of Chichester consecrated the church on 14 May 1959. There is a plaque inside relating to the fact that there was no loss of life during WWI with the inscription: -

East Wittering beach.

1914–1918 No lives were lost
from this Parish.
All returned safely.

WEST WITTERING

West Wittering is a village situated on the Manhood Peninsula near the mouth of Chichester Harbour. It is part of a Site of Special Interest and is very famous for its soft white sandy beaches which have been described as having excellent water quality. Chichester Harbour, a Site of Special Scientific Interest is partly within the parish. As we have already seen this is a wetland of international importance, a Special Protection Area for wild birds and a Special Area of Conservation. For most people

The famous soft white sand of West Wittering beach.

West Wittering means one thing – the beach – and what a beach it is. I can personally confirm that whenever it is a hot day the A286 from Chichester to the Manhood Peninsula is clogged, sometimes at a standstill with day trippers and holiday makers heading for West Wittering. The large car parks become full, the

Roped off pathway through sand dunes that are stabilised with marram grass.

West Wittering beach.

beaches packed and people enjoying the sea; it is one of the most popular beaches in south-east England. The beach has gently shelving sands and there are views to the Isle of Wight and Hayling Island. As you look out across the English Channel you will notice how busy it can get with major shipping; freight ships are regularly passing each other as they go around the Isle of Wight missing the many small sailing yachts that enjoy this area.

As you approach West Wittering beach from East Wittering you climb a roped off path through sand dunes which is great fun for children and most adults. The area is a sand dune and marram grass regeneration area and the marram grass (Ammophila) is planted as it helps stabilise the dunes. These grasses are found almost exclusively on the first line of coastal sand dunes and their system of creeping underground stems allow them to thrive under conditions of shifting sands and high winds, thus helping to stabilize and prevent coastal erosion. The grasses are known as plants that can withstand dry conditions despite their location on sea coasts. It is for this reason that the plants have been introduced here although they are native to the coasts of the North Atlantic Ocean where they are the dominant species on dunes.

East Head.

The Spit.

East Head is a sand spit about a mile long which curves in towards the middle of Chichester Harbour and it was this area that was visible from Cobnor bird hide at Chidham that you visited on Walk 2. East Head spit joins the mainland at a narrow strip of sand called The Hinge. Although this area is partly sheltered by the Isle of Wight The Hinge takes the full force of the wind and waves and there is a real risk that one day the sea might break through The Hinge, cutting off East Head and destroying the salt marsh behind it. Between the spit of East Head and the mainland there is a sheltered lagoon which is an important habitat. The wetland salt marsh has plants including purslane, sea lavender and eel grass.

WEST ITCHENOR

West Itchenor is a village on the Manhood Peninsula that lies on the shores of Chichester Harbour and when you sat on the bench at Cobnor Point in Chidham on Walk 2, West Itchenor was the closest point to you. The name Itchenor originates from a Saxon chieftain called Icca who settled here around the time of Roman Britain and it was originally known as Iccannore ('Icca's shore'); it is still officially called West Itchenor despite East Itchenor disappearing in the fifteenth century. A settlement is thought to have been established here during the Roman conquest of Britain in AD43, however the area was one of the first to be resettled by the South Saxons when they colonised the south coast. The Domesday Book of 1086 names the village as Icenore, in 1187 it was called Ichenore and by 1243 Westichenor. The Domesday Book also mentions that Icenore was held by 'Warin', a henchman of 'Earl Roger' who invaded England with William the Conqueror. The manor later became a parcel (plot of land) of the Earl of Arundel.

In 1175 the Lord of the Manor, Hugh Esturmy, built a chapel in West Itchenor that was adjacent to the Haven and prior to the construction of a sea wall and sluice in 1931 a spring tide would cause the river to rise and surround the building. Between 1180 and 1197 the chapel became a parish church which was dedicated to St Nicholas the patron saint of seafarers.

St. Nicholas church.

During the Black Death which swept England from 1348 the population of West Itchenor diminished yet the village survived. East Itchenor its neighbouring village did not survive and its subsequent decline in the following century culminated in its unification with Birdham in 1440 after

West Itchenor.

which it became farming land. The loss of East Itchenor was also the result of siltation (water pollution caused by particulate terrestrial clastic material, with a particle size dominated by silt or clay) in the harbour, which made West Itchenor the more viable port location.

Near the end of the nineteenth century West Itchenor become a popular destination for Londoners who were able to afford a second home in the countryside. Known locally as 'DFLs' (Down from London) these people caused the rapid growth of the village and in 2012 the Itchenor Society estimated that in 2012 over 40% of all households were second homes.

During WWII, Itchenor Shipyard served as a base for the Admiralty's manufacturing of Fairmile B motor launches and Itchenor Sailing Club was requisitioned by the British Army, which mounted an anti-aircraft gun at the club to attack approaching Luftwaffe planes. This meant that West Itchenor became a restricted area and required that all residents produce identification papers when entering the village.

Since the 1700s shipbuilding has been the main source of employment within the village and it was the site of a prominent shipyard during the Napoleonic Wars from which a number of warships were launched including HMS *Pelorus* in 1808 and HMS *Curacao* in 1809. In 1800 the Transit, a 101ft long, four-masted barquentine (or schooner – a sailing vessel with three or more masts; with a square rigged foremast and fore-and-aft rigged main, mizzen and any other masts) weighing 200 tons was built here and is said to have been revolutionary in the design of its hull and rig. During the nineteenth century, construction started to decline due to the development of railways which provided a more accessible mode of transport. Shipbuilding made a modern revival with the opening of Haines boatyard in 1912. In 1936 a new ship yard called the 'Itchenor Shipyard' was built on the site that had seen production during the eighteenth and nineteenth centuries. Northshore Yachts Ltd now occupies the site and has overseen the complete manufacturing of Fisher and Southerly yachts since the mid-1970s.

West Itchenor boatyard.

The Ship Inn.

Itchenor Sailing Club.

Itchenor Sailing Club was founded in 1927 and since then it has hosted national and local sailing competitions, including annual events such as Schools Week and Junior Fortnight. It is recognised as a Royal Yachting Association Volvo Champion Club and has produced a number of successful Olympic sailors.

The Ship Inn is a lovely pub that I use whenever I am walking in this area. Rebuilt in 1933 it is located in the heart of the village about 50 yards from Chichester Harbour. On hot days the pub gets very busy with walkers, cyclists and sailors who take advantage of the outdoor seating area.

Now that you know what to expect, you can do Walk 4. I will see you in Chapter 5 where we will visit the coastline at Bracklesham Bay and explore Medmerry RSPB Nature Reserve.

SUGGESTED WALK

WALK 4. East Wittering, West Wittering and West Itchenor
(9 miles 14.5 km)

Parking. There is roadside parking in Culimore Road or other nearby side roads. (Post code PO20 8HB.) Alternatively, there is a pay-and-display car park in Marine Drive. This is a long but lovely walk with so many views. It starts along East Wittering beach which then goes directly into the beautiful sandy beaches of West Wittering via sand dunes which you have to climb. Here you can visit The Spit and East Head before continuing beside Chichester Harbour to reach West Itchenor with all its yachts. The walk is generally flat and there are no stiles but you do have to walk across pebbles on East Wittering beach which can be a bit strenuous. There are many viewing benches throughout this walk for a rest.

For me, if you are doing these walks in order from west to east, this is the most useful walk so far. From previous walks you will have looked across to Portsmouth, Hayling Island and Emsworth and you will have walked beside Thorney Channel, Bosham Channel and Chichester Channel. On this walk you will see all of these places and with binoculars or a zoom camera you will be able to see or photograph the places that you have already walked. Allow plenty of time for this walk and try to understand the exact layout of Chichester Harbour; I have made reference to all of these places during the walk. There are numerous places for refreshments including the Shore Inn at the start, the Ship Inn at West Itchenor and the Lamb Inn which is ideally located on the return route by which time you may have worked up a thirst.

East Wittering beach with the Isle of Wight and Portsmouth ahead.

Sand dunes as you approach West Wittering beach.

1. From the lower house number end of Culimore Road go left along Marine Drive and follow it past a green on the left and then a pay-and-display car park (alternative parking area). At the end, go right down Shore Road, not signed, and near the end you reach the Shore Inn on the right.

The Shore Inn at the start of the walk.

Fisherman's Hut on East Wittering beach.

East Wittering beach.

2. From the pub, continue down Shore Road to the beach where you turn right by the Fisherman's Hut and walk along the concrete path. Soon the path ends and you have to continue along the top of the pebble beach; from this area you have a good view of the Isle of Wight and a distant view of the Spinnaker Tower at Portsmouth ahead. Just follow the beach along concrete, pebbles or grass ignoring any of the exits on the right. As you walk into a grassy area, with your view of the sea obscured you start to get the sense that you are starting to walk on sand and then you climb sand dunes following a roped-off path to arrive at the famous and very popular sandy West Wittering beach – no pebbles. Continue along the top of the beach, passing beach huts on the right with a large visitor car park behind them. Just keep going to the end of the beach where there are a few more pebbles and now you have arrived at the start of The Spit and East Head.

Start of the sandy West Wittering beach.

Heading towards The Spit.

The Spit/East Head.

38

When you reach a beacon, the onward path has now been blocked off due to erosion so a few yards before the beacon go right to a car park then go left to the end of the car park where you reach The Spit. From the end of the car park you can clearly see the layout of The Spit, East Head, The Hinge and the salt marsh within this area. From this point you can also see the Isle of Wight, Hayling Island and Thorney Island and you are now standing at the entrance to Chichester Harbour. You can go and explore The Spit and East Head as an optional detour but my walk continues to West Itchenor which is still a few miles away.

3. At the end of the car park turn right and follow the path that is to the left of the wooden barriers/fence; just follow this path, enjoying the views of East Head as you go. When you cross a bridge and the path bends to the left you have arrived at Snow Hill; keep left here and in a few yards, you reach a 4-way footpath sign. Keep left and follow the enclosed path, between the rear of houses and the Thorney Channel, as it winds its way offering some open views of the harbour as you go. Soon the path opens up and you continue around to the right with good views.

View at Snow Hill.

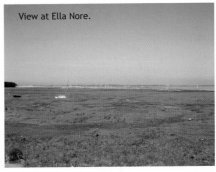

View at Ella Nore.

At a bird hide the path bends to the right, you are now at Ella Nore. (From here you are looking out across the Thorney Channel and can see Hayling Island, Thorney Island and Chidham.) Continue following the path, go through a gate and immediately go left through another gate and continue beside the harbour. At a 2-way footpath sign, with a wide wooden gate on the left, go right as directed, then left and ahead through a swing gate, beside a house called Camber Court, and follow the enclosed path back to the harbour. Now just continue, ignoring any side paths and crossing a few basic bridges as you go. As you go along this long path look out for the Thorney Island Sailing Club on Thorney Island and the wooden steps you walked down at Chidham on to the flooded beach near Cobnor Point; the sailing club is easier to see.

After what seems like forever, you reach Haines boatyard. Walk directly ahead across the boatyard and continue along the enclosed path on the other side. On the far side you reach the Harbour Office at West Itchenor, here you can go on Harbour Tours around Chichester Harbour. Turn right up The Street, not signed and in about

View towards West Itchenor.

West Itchenor boatyard.

50 yards you reach the Ship Inn on the right for well-deserved refreshments. (From this area you can look out across the Chichester Channel to Cobnor Point at Chidham with the Bosham Channel to the right of Chidham and Thorney Channel to the left of Chidham. With the exception of a short walk along the Fishbourne Channel on Walk 8 near Apuldram this is the end of our exploration of Chichester Harbour.)

The Lamb Inn for welcome refreshment.

4. From the pub continue along The Street and just follow the fairly quiet road soon passing St Nicholas church on the left and a pond on the right. Continue along what has now become Itchenor Road, ignoring any side roads or footpaths and at a main road junction go right signposted to Witterings. Follow the road and in a short distance, where it curves to the right, go almost directly ahead along a footpath on the left as directed by a footpath sign (this is on the bend and Hallowtide house is opposite). Follow the path which can get a little overgrown, cross a wooden bridge and at the end you reach a main road. (Turn left along the road for a few yards if you would like refreshments at the Lamb Inn on the left).

5. To continue the walk, turn right along the main road using the right-hand grass verge. When you reach Itchenor Road, cross (left) over the main road and go along Piggery Hall Lane opposite. At a road junction, go right along Acre Street. At the end, go left down Chapel Lane, not signed, and when the road curves right, go left through a wide opening as directed by a footpath sign. Follow the obvious path across a large field, cross a bridge and continue directly ahead across a field. On the far side, go ahead along a concrete path through Scotts Farm camping site. Just keep going ahead along the concrete path and access road to reach a road at the end. Turn left and go along the road using the right-hand pavement and just before a sign for East Wittering, go right down The Crescent. At the end by house No.39 go right along a 'T' road, pass between a barrier and follow Culimore Road ahead and around to the left back to the start.

CHAPTER 5

BRACKLESHAM BAY & MEDMERRY RSPB NATURE RESERVE

Medmerry RSPB Nature Reserve.

Kestrel at Medmerry RSPB Nature Reserve.

BRACKLESHAM BAY

Bracklesham Bay is a Site of Special Scientific Interest. It is a coastal bay on the west side of the Manhood Peninsula that looks out across the English Channel to the Isle of Wight. The bay is bordered by Bracklesham, which is an ever incresing expanse of residential properties, to the west and Selsey to the east.

Bracklesham Bay is a predominantly shingle beach which becomes sandier as the tide goes out, it also exposes wooden groynes which disappear again when the tide comes back in. Although partially sheltered by the Isle of Wight, strong winds and currents driving up the English Channel from the southwest mean continuous protection is needed to preserve the coastline. The strong winds make Bracklesham Bay one of the south coast's leading centres for windsurfing and other board sports. It is also an ideal place for fossil hunting and 'sharks teeth' are particularly common.

Bracklesham gives its name to a geological feature, the Bracklesham Beds, which are a mixture of clays and marls that run from here through to southern Hampshire and the Isle of Wight. The Bracklesham Beds are good for fossil hunting and as well as the 'sharks teeth' the fossil bearing rocks of the Bracklesham coast have yielded fossil molluscs, corals, sea snakes and fish. The fossils date to the Eocene era around 46 million years ago. This stretch of shoreline has unimproved grazing pastures, shingle, salt marsh, reed beds and ditches. The pasture is subject to seasonal flooding making it important for its breeding and overwintering birds. In May 1944, in preparation for D-Day, Canadian soldiers practiced an amphibious landing on this beach; the remains of a tank from that operation can still be found underwater.

Bracklesham Bay towards the Witterings

Various habitats within Medmerry RSPB Nature Reserve.

The earth embankment at Medmerry holding back the sea was originally built in the 1960s but the coastline was subject to frequent flooding events which were becoming unsustainable. The Medmerry managed realignment scheme arose out of consultations from the 2008 Pagham to East Head Coastal Defence Strategy and the Medmerry realignment project was completed in 2013 at a cost of £28m. It is the largest open-coast scheme in Europe and one of the most sustainable projects the Enviroment Agency has ever delivered. The project provides 1000 times better flood protection than the prevoius defence system and has delivered extensive new intertidal and freshwater habitat, compensating for losses elsewhere in the region caused by coastal squeeze. Managed realignment is an environmental management approach that involves altering the location of the line of defence, working to provide a more sustainable position from which to manage flood and erosion risks. It can involve advancement (moving forward), set back or breach of the existing defence line but most often it involves a new set back line of defence on the coast or within an estuary.

Coastal flooding has long been a problem at Medmerry and it posed a serious risk to the nearby towns of Selsey and Pagham. The previous defence, a 3km shingle bank, was subject to regular sea breaches the most recent being in 2008 when over £5m of damage was caused. As well as offering a deficient level of protection the old shingle bank's maintenance which was largely done through constant re-profiling throughout the winter using bulldozers, had become costly and unsustainable and the Environment Agency was spending up to £300,000 a year for its upkeep. A wider issue in the region of the Solent is the loss of important coastal habitat as a result of coastal squeeze. The impacts of development and flood defence infrastructure around the large urbanised areas of Southampton and Portsmouth have caused local sea levels to rise and wetland and intertidal habitats to be lost to the sea. The Medmerry scheme is the first site in the region to offer large-scale provision of compensatory habitat.

Fundamental to the scheme was the creation of a breach in the existing shingle bank to allow the sea to reclaim the area of land close to the shore. New floodbanks were built around the perimeter of the new flood inundation zone and while they sit much closer to the surrounding communities than the previous shingle bank, the result is significantly increased flood protection. The inundation zone absorbs the energy and impact of the waves while also offering new habitat.

Sustainable and environmentally friendly approaches were adopted throughout construction. Much of the rock was delivered directly to the site by sea to reduce the impact on local roads and access tracks were built from recycled materials. Ground nesting birds were protected from construction impacts by using an innovative cropping regime which was devised by the RSPB and local farmers and it was so successful that no construction phases were delayed because of nesting birds. The scheme was completed in late 2013, the construction having taken a total of 62 weeks, and it immediately proved its worth by successfully protecting local communities from flooding during storms that winter. A total of 348 properties, a sewage works, caravan parks and Selsey's main road route are now protected to a standard of 1 in 100 years, previously it was just 1 in 1 year. Birds and other new wildlife began to appear at the site long before completion.

Medmerry RSPB Nature Reserve is described as a 'wild and wonderful' reserve with no facilities or hides. It is a vast site which has been made as accessible as possible given its restraints. As a site of national importance for wildlife it is recognised as a Site of Special Scientific interest (SSSI). The site contains 300 hectares of habitat of principal importance under the UK Biodiversity Action Plan and includes mudflats, reed beds, saline lagoons and grassland. It includes 183 hectares of newly created intertidal habitat important to wildlife on an international level and allows the region to meet its European directive targets.

Now you can do the there-and-back walk through Medmerry Nature Reserve looking out for the varied wildlife. I will see you in Selsey, my home town.

SUGGESTED WALK

WALK 5. Medmerry RSPB Nature Reserve (3 miles 4.8 km)

Parking. There is a small RSPB Nature Reserve car park along Easton Lane - it is signed but is easy to miss. If you arrive from Almodington Lane it is on the right, if you are heading towards Almodington Lane it is on the left. On busy days, like warm weekends, the car park can get full but it has a fairly quick turnover. (Postcode PO20 7NU nearest.) This is a short there-and-back walk through the newest Nature Reserve that is the result of one of the largest flood risk management schemes of its kind ever undertaken in Britain. There are viewing benches so take your binoculars or zoom camera for the birdlife. There are no places for refreshments.

1. From the free RSPB car park go through the swing gate beside the RSPB information board and go across the bridge which has wooden sides to reach a junction. There are two paths to your right that are close together, the lower wider one is a cycle path and the narrower one to the left of it is a footpath; these paths run parallel to each other all the way through the reserve to the beach. Take the footpath which starts up a slight incline as there is less chance of getting hit by a cyclist and just follow it going through swing gates as you go. As you go keep a lookout for butterflies and dragonflies.

Footpath parallel to cycle path.

As you walk along there is one very minor loop on the left where there are two conveniently placed viewing benches where you may see Canada geese or other birdlife. As you continue there are ponds and lagoons all around you including on the opposite side of the cycle path so keep a look out over there as well; if you are lucky you may see a kestrel just sitting on a post.

When you reach the beach the first two things you will probably notice are the Isle of Wight in front of you and numerous warning signs saying 'No beach access beyond this point'; this area floods, has soft uneven ground and strong currents. From where you are you get good views of Selsey to the left including Medmerry windmill which you will visit in the next chapter, Bracklesham to the right and beyond Bracklesham in the distance is the Spinnaker Tower at Portsmouth in Hampshire.

2. After appreciating the views and maybe doing a bit of fossil hunting on the beach, return the same way; you may prefer to use the cycle path so that you get a better view of the ponds and lagoons on the left but just be careful of the cyclists especially if you have children with you. Unfortunately, due to the layout of the Nature Reserve there is no way to devise a circular walk.

CHAPTER 6
SELSEY & CHURCH NORTON

Medmerry (Selsey) Windmill.

Selsey and Church Norton are very much inter-related and for the purpose of this book are going to be considered as one. Selsey is a seaside town located at the tip of the Manhood Peninsula and Selsey Bill is the southernmost tip of West Sussex. It is bounded to the west by Brackleham Bay, Broad Rife to the north (rife is a local word for stream or creek) and Pagham Harbour to the east. There are rock formations off both of its coasts named the Owers rocks and Mixon rocks and it was a base for Sir Francis Drake's men who tried to lure the Spanish Armada on to Owers rocks. The B2145 is the only road in and out of the town and it crosses a bridge over the water inlet at Pagham Harbour at a point known as 'The Ferry' (Chapter 7). At one time Selsey was inaccessible at flood tide and a boat was stationed at The Ferry to take horses and passengers to and from Siddlesham. The tiny village of Church Norton is to the east of Selsey and has a boundary with Pagham Harbour Nature Reserve.

Selsey Lifeboat Day – spraying children on the beach.

Selsey was cited as the capital of the Kingdom of Sussex c680, it was mentioned in the Domesday Book and has historically been a fishing community. The town is dominated by the sea as it always has been and is popular with fishermen and famous for its Selsey crab and lobsters; Selsey still has its own fishing fleet. The beaches are generally shingle interspersed with wooden groynes. According to Bede the name Selsey is derived from the Saxon Seals-ey and can be interpreted as the Isle of Sea Calves (sea calves are better known as seals). Edward Heron-Allen (an English polymath, writer, scientist and Persian scholar 1861-1943) identified at least twenty different spellings of the place now known as Selsey including Seoles – Old English, Seleisie – Domesday Book 1086, and Celesye – Assize Roll 1279.

Selsey beach towards Bognor.

Selsey beach towards Medmerry Nature Reserve.

The earliest evidence of human habitation in the Selsey area dates back to the Stone Age; various stone implements have been found which date to the Palaeolithic period. Selsey was the capital of the Kingdom of Sussex and was possibly founded by Ælle (recorded in early sources as the first king of the South Saxons, reigning in what is now called Sussex from 477 to c514). Wilfrid arrived c680 and converted the kingdom to Christianity as is recorded by the Venerable Bede. Selsey Abbey stood at Selsey, possibly where Church Norton is today, and it was the cathedral for the Sussex Diocese until the Council of London ordered the removal of the See to Chichester in 1075, during the reign of William the Conqueror. The manor of Selsey remained with the Bishop of Chichester until 1561 when it was taken over by the crown.

Over the centuries whilst Selsey has made an income from the sea, one of the enterprises was smuggling. In the eighteenth century Selsey Bill was more isolated than it is today and the sand spit extended farther out to sea. Only the causeway connected to the mainland and that was covered at high tide so the approach of the local riding officer (a person who patrolled the coast for smuggling) would have been very conspicuous. The Rectors of Selsey reputedly claimed a tithe on all the kegs landed here and stories also tell of a passageway leading from the Old Rectory at Church Norton to the remains of a mound, which is thought to have been built by the Normans; the course of the tunnel was marked by a depression on the surface of the ground as late as 1911. In the 1720s one Selsey man ran a regular ferry service to France going back and forth every five weeks and other prominent Selsey figures made considerable fortunes just from part-time work in the free trade.

In 1749 fourteen smugglers who were members of the notorious Hawkhurst Gang were accused of the murder of Mr William Galley who was a custom-house officer and Daniel Chater who was a shoemaker. Seven of the gang were tried and condemned to death at Chichester assizes (periodic courts held around England and Wales until 1972), one died in jail before sentence could be carried out and the other six were hung at Broyle, north of Chichester. Subsequently the bodies of John Cobby and John Hammond were then hung in gibbets (any instrument of public execution including hanging gallows) at Gibbet Field at Selsey Bill so that they could be seen at great distance from the east and west. There is a blue plaque along the seafront commemorating this event which is passed on Walk 6.

Selsey was connected to Chichester from 1897 to 1935 by a rail link that was initially called the Hundred of Manhood and Selsey Tramway and later the West Sussex Railway. The light railway rolling stock was all second hand, very unreliable and journey times were long leading to various nicknames including the 'Selsey Snail'. (This railway is described in more detail in Chapter 7 as it also ran through Pagham Nature Reserve.)

Notable Selsey residents include Eric Coates 1886-1957 who was an English composer who lived and worked in Selsey. He was inspired to write 'By the Sleepy Lagoon' after overlooking the sea towards Bognor Regis and his musical

GIBBET FIELD
AS A WARNING TO OTHERS
THE BODIES OF
TWO SMUGGLERS
EXECUTED IN 1749
WERE HUNG IN CHAINS
FROM THE GIBBET
THAT STOOD IN THIS FIELD
MUCH OF WHICH NOW
UNDER THE SEA

Gibbet Field plaque.

composition can be heard as the theme tune to *Desert Island Discs*. You will pass a blue plaque on the seafront dedicated to him on Walk 7. Sir Patrick Moore 1923-2012 who was a famous TV astronomer who presented *The Sky at Night* from 1957, writer, researcher and radio commentator lived in Selsey from 1968 until his death in 2012.

St Peter's church in Selsey has a very interesting history. It was founded by St Wilfrid over thirteen centuries ago but today it it stands in two parts: one, the old chancel which is now known as St Wilfrid's Chapel at Church Norton and the other, the parish church of St Peter. In the mid-nineteenth century, the growing population of Selsey found it inconvenient to have the parish church situated some 2 miles away and so it was decided to demolish the church at church Norton and re-erect it, stone-by-stone on its present site. Under ecclesiastical law a church may be moved but not its chancel – hence the rare anomaly of having a church in

St Peter's Church.

two parts. The demolition began in November 1864 and the stones and pillars were transported on farm carts to the new site together with the oak roof with its king and queen posts. The project took eighteen months to complete and the re-erected church incorporating the late twelfth century arcades of three bays of the original building, with new chancel and vestry was consecrated on 12 April 1866; it is now a Grade II listed building.

St Wilfrid's Chapel at Church Norton now resembles a chapel in the middle of a cemetery. Only the chancel from the old church remains but this church in this setting is full of character and charm. Inside there is a monument of John Lewis (d1537) and his wife Agnes made of Caen stone. Beneath a depressed canopy, which has lost its cresting, the figures kneel either side of a blank space, where there would have been a representation of the Trinity or the Risen Christ. The inscription is in scrolls above the figures and behind them are small representations of St George and the dragon and the Martyrdom of St Agatha. On the chest are quatrefoils enclosing shields. Both of these churches are visited on Walk 7.

Selsey is famous for its lifeboat station and it is a case of the old and new. Local residents as well as previous visitors to Selsey will remember the old iconic lifeboat station that was built in 1925 where the offshore lifeboat was launched down a ramp from a boat house at the end of a pier. A new station was built onshore in 2016 and enabled all the elements of the RNLI to come together under one roof on a single site. On 1 April 2017 the station's Tyne Class Lifeboat *Voluntary Worker* was launched down the slipway from the old boathouse for the last time, to be kept at moorings until it was replaced by the new Shannon Class Lifeboat during the summer; the Shannon is carriage launched across the beach from the new boathouse. The old station and pier were demolished and removed in July 2017 and the seabed returned to its natural state; *Voluntary Worker* was returned to Poole HQ in July 2017. The new station now comprises of *Denise and Eric* which is a Shannon Class Lifeboat and *Flt Lt John Buckley RAF* which is a 'D' Class Lifeboat. A lifeboat station was first established here in 1861 and in 2011 they celebrated 150 years during which time the lifeboat crew have received ten awards for gallantry. Each year there is a Selsey Lifeboat Week culminating with a Sunday launch day, usually the first Sunday in August. The lifeboat crews compete in a raft race against other entrants and put on displays with

St Wilfrid's Chapel.

49

St Wilfrid's Chapel.

Monument of John Lewis and wife Agnes.

rescue helicopters etc. The fun ends when anybody sitting next to the sea gets sprayed by the lifeboat crew; you've been warned but children love it. The lifeboat station is passed on Walk 6.

Another well-known landmark in Selsey is Medmerry Windmill (Selsey Windmill); it is a Grade II listed tower mill which has been restored and is now a well-known feature especially for holidaymakers arriving at the caravan park. It was built around 1827,

Old lifeboat station.

replacing an earlier post mill and was working by wind until 1890. After falling into disrepair, it was refitted by Holloway of Shoreham in 1907-08 and continued working until the early 1920s. By 1928 the mill was derelict with all four sails badly damaged. The fan stage was removed in 1960 during the restoration of the mill and in the storm of 1987 the mill was badly damaged but the sails were later restored. Walk 6 takes you to the windmill.

In 2012 work was undertaken to improve the flood defences at West Beach to help protect the caravan park. The work was privately funded by the caravan park at a cost of £16.8m. The large granite rocks that form the breakwaters are clearly visible and are popular locations with beach fishermen. The project aimed to construct two temporary causeways which would enable the building of two

New lifeboat station.

offshore breakwaters each with a 2-acre footprint (two football pitches). The beach would then be built up between the two breakwaters which are 610m apart and the temporary causeways would be removed after the breakwaters were completed. To do the work 93,000 tonnes of granite rocks were brought in by ship from the Larvik Quarry in Norway. The cores of the breakwaters were built from 0.3 to 1 tonne rocks, while the outer or 'armour' layers were built from six to 10 tonne rocks. The beach was then restored and enlarged with half a million tonnes of sand and shingle. In a process called 'shingle beach recharge' 115 ships each brought in 3000m^3 of sand and shingle that was pumped through a pipe leading from the dredger to the beach; the sand and shingle was then profiled by bulldozers to form the beach.

As you enter the town of Selsey you are welcomed by 'The Wave' which is a work of art also called Kanagawa that sits beside a small roundabout; Kanagawa is an area of Honshu Island in Japan. The sculptor William Pye has taken its name for the title of this sculpture based on the famous wood-block print of a wave by the artist Katsuhika Hokusai (1760-1849). The Hollow of the Deep Sea Wave off Kanagawa, became the subject for this sculpture, which is also known simply as 'The Wave'. The sculpture is made of bronze and weighs about 2.5 tonnes. The Wave is passed at the end of Walk 7.

Now you can do the two walks associated with Selsey and Church Norton and I will see you at Pagham where we explore the Nature Reserves.

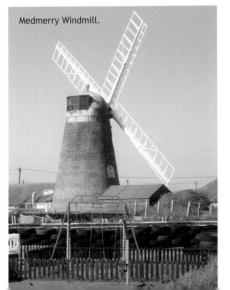

Medmerry Windmill.

Completed sea defences.

SUGGESTED WALK

WALK 6. Selsey Lifeboat Station and Medmerry Windmill (4 miles 6.4 km)

Parking. On-street parking in Kingsway beside the green or in another side road (Post code PO20 0DL.) There is also a pay-and-display car park at the far end of Kingsway. This is a fairly short walk with no significant hills. There are two short sections along the beach on pebbles but no stiles. There are various places for refreshments including the Lifeboat Inn at the start/finish, The Seal, convenience store beside Medmerry Windmill or various shops in the High Street.

1. Go along the road with the large green on your left. Soon you reach the new lifeboat station which was built in 2016 to replace the old station that was a well-known landmark for Selsey and for the purposes of nostalgia, I have included a photo for the old lifeboat station as well. From the lifeboat station walk up to reach the concrete path at the top of the beach. Turn right and just follow the path, soon passing a memorial, on a grassy area, to two smugglers who were hung at Gibbet Field.

Pier to access the old lifeboat station.

Lifeboat in new on-shore station.

The path ends turn right up the access road and in 20 yards turn left beside Bill Cottage. In 25 yards keep to the right of the buildings and go ahead to reach the beach. Turn right along a gravel path and pass a line of viewing benches. On the far side you reach an access road on the right by a barrier. Go left on to the beach for 5 yards then go up a concrete bank and continue along the coastal path passing the remains of some coastal defences built in 1953. Go ahead along the path, walking on pebbles, and follow it until you reach Hillfield Road pay-and-display car park.

Old coastal defences.

New coastguard's tower.

2. At the far side of the car park, by its entrance, turn right up Hillfield Road, not signed, and soon you turn left along Clayton Road. Just follow Clayton Road to its end ignoring all the side roads. At the end of this long road you arrive at a 'T' junction where you turn left along West Street; there is a house sign on the wall opposite that shows West Street. Go down the road to reach the new coastguard's radio tower on the right. Immediately after the tower, go right along a wide gravel drive next to Lands End Cottage. In 20 yards go left between a barrier and follow the raised coastal path with Medmerry Windmill in view over to the right.

Follow the path and at a footpath sign, when the windmill is almost directly on your right, go right along the narrow path beside a wire fence on the right heading towards the windmill. Pass a crazy golf course on the left (the crazy golf course may be removed as the caravan park has recently been bought by an American company who want to develop this area) and continue out to reach Medmerry Windmill by the entrance to the caravan park.

3. At the windmill turn right down Mill Lane. Follow the lane past caravans on the left and continue until Mill Lane bends to the right into Crablands; it is not signed but, in a few yards, you pass Crablands Close on the left. Continue along Crablands passing Paddock Lane on the left and at the next junction go left along West Street immediately passing a house named The Forge on the right. Follow the road out to the High Street.

4. Turn right down the High Street (the main High Street is to your left) and in about 35 yards, opposite The Seal pub on the right, go left along Latham Road. Keep straight ahead as Latham Road automatically goes into Grove Road, not signed, and at the end of Grove Road cross a road and go directly ahead along a concrete path beside three concrete bollards. In a few yards, cross a road and continue ahead along an enclosed public footpath. Just go ahead along the path until you reach the Lifeboat Inn at the end. This is my local pub so if you see me in there, say hello and mine's a Guinness.

Turn left at the pub and in 15 yards go right into Kingsway back to the start.

Medmerry Windmill.

The Lifeboat Inn.

SUGGESTED WALK

WALK 7. St Peters Church and St Wilfrid's Chapel (5 miles 8 km)

Parking. On-street parking near the church (Post code PO20 0NP.) This is a flat walk but there is one long section along pebbles on the beach that can be strenuous and one stile. There are no places for refreshments on this walk.

1. With your back to the church, go left along Chichester Road to the mini roundabout in view. Pass the roundabout and continue ahead along Chichester Road passing St Peter's Crescent on the left. In about 50 yards cross over the main road to a bus shelter on the opposite side and continue along Chichester Road for a few yards passing a blue plaque for the Selsey Tramway and then in a few more yards go right along a wide concrete path.

Stained glass in porch. St Peter's church.

Selsey Tramway plaque.

Follow the path through a small park out to Manor Road, not signed, by barriers at the end with the Selsey Centre on your left. Cross the road and continue ahead along another concrete path which you follow to its end where it reaches Manor Lane, not signed. Go left along the residential road and when the left-hand pavement ends continue along the right-hand pavement until you reach Drift Road at the end. Continue directly ahead along a gravel access road and follow it until you reach a junction of access roads with Park Farm opposite (this is where you will come out on your return journey). Turn right along the access road and follow it, soon passing houses, to reach the beach at the end. At the very edge of the beach look for a blue plaque on the left to Eric Coates who composed 'By The Sleepy Lagoon' in 1930 which was later used as the signature tune for the BBC's *Desert Island Discs*. This view was his inspiration.

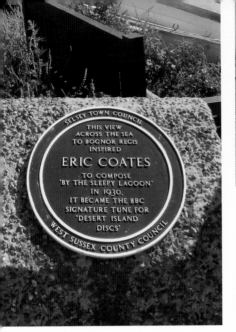
Eric Coates plaque.

Beach on the way to Church Norton.

Pagham Harbour Nature Reserve at Church Norton.

2. Turn left along the beach now walking on pebbles with a good view of Bognor Regis ahead with the white conical tent-like structure of Butlin's Holiday Park (Chapter 9). Follow the beach past all the seafront houses and about 30 yards past the last house continue ahead to the left of a long wooden barrier that from a distance looks like a bridge.

Pass a lake on the left which is good for bird watching and when the wooden barrier ends continue ahead along the upper part of the beach with part of the bird reserve on your left. Just follow the path ahead, ignoring a footpath sign to the left, and when the path starts to curve around to the right go left down a row of 'sleeper' boards to a wire fence.

Continue with the wire fence on your left and keep a look out for the many species of birds in this area as you are now at Pagham Harbour Nature Reserve. At the end of the wire fence you reach a 3-way signpost by an information board. Ignore this left turn and continue ahead. Keep to the left beside the trees and follow the path along wooden walkways and paths which can get muddy and slippery so take care. Pass Church Norton bird hide and just after the second wooden walkway the path reaches a section of small stones; continue for 20 yards then go left up wooden steps. At the top of the steps go left and follow the enclosed path to reach the rear entrance to St Wilfrid's Chapel at Church Norton. Go over the stone steps and ahead to reach the chapel.

St Wilfrid's Chapel.

3. Leave the chapel and go out through the main lych gate into the gravel car park. Go ahead along the uneven lane and soon it bends around to the right up Rectory Lane, not signed. Follow the lane until you reach Pigeon House Farm Lane on the left; there is also a Public Footpath sign. Go left here and just follow the uneven road passing a number of farm buildings along the way.

When you eventually reach an access road on the right by a white gate (this will be obvious) and a high pole on the left with five surveillance cameras on it, continue ahead for 25 yards along a right field edge to reach a 3-way footpath sign. Continue ahead along the field edge path with a wooden fence and trees on your right. In the field corner the path bends to the right by a gate and you follow the path as indicated by a marker post; now heading towards Park Farm in front of you. Follow the path then access drive passing the farm buildings on your left out to the access road you used earlier.

Turn right up the uneven track and follow it to reach Chichester Road at the end. Cross the road and turn left along the pavement to reach 'The Wave' roundabout which welcomes visitors to Selsey. There is an information board here with details about 'The Wave'. Just keep going ahead along Chichester Road until you eventually arrive back at St Peter's church on the right.

'The Wave' welcomes you to Selsey.

CHAPTER 7
PAGHAM

Dipping pond at Pagham RSPB Nature Reserve.

Pagham is a semi-rural coastal village that sits on the edge of Pagham Harbour. Over the centuries the area now occupied by Pagham Harbour has gone between successful attempts to reclaim it as farmland, followed by disaster when the sea decided that it wanted the harbour back. The shallow waters of Pagham Harbour are a valuable Nature Reserve and although it may not be as well populated by birds as Chichester Harbour, which is a much larger expanse of water, it is still very popular with bird watchers. It is also a great place to walk and to get a good idea of the awesome power of nature.

Pagham Harbour is a Site of Special Scientific Interest and the harbour and surrounding land is of national importance for both flora and fauna. The shingle spit is of geological interest. Roughly half of the reserve is intertidal saltmarsh and mudflats with the remainder of the reserve consisting of farmland, copses, reedbeds and shingle beaches. The saltmarsh and mudflats are an intertidal area that supports invertebrates including ragworms, snails, shrimps and crabs which in turn form the staple diet of many wading birds that are attracted to this site in

Cross the sluice to reach the North Wall at Pagham Harbour Nature Reserve.

The North Wall.

Typical view of the Nature Reserve.

their droves. There are specialist plants that are able to cope with the tidal influx which also provide food for ducks, geese and finches. The areas of grassland and farmland consist mainly of permanent grass which provides valuable feeding for waders at high tide and grazing for winter ducks and geese. Hedgerow and scrub offer cover, food and nest sites, while set-aside is used by ground-nesters.

Shingle and vegetated shingle are popular for breeding shorebirds including little terns and ringed plovers which make shallow scrapes on the shingle spits and islands. The vegetated shingle also provides a home for yellow-horned poppy, sea kale and the nationally scarce childing pink, which can only be found on two sites along all of the south coast. The reedbed and lagoons are a mix of reedbed and fresh, salt and saline lagoons which attract a variety of birds, animals and insects. In summer as you walk around the harbour on the two associated walks, look out for butterflies that flit along the hedgerows, dragonflies over ponds and lizards basking in the sun. In winter there are large flocks of migratory birds such as Brent geese and pintails.

One of the more unusual parts of the Nature Reserve is Pagham Lagoon which lies between the sea and Church Farm Holiday Park where some lucky caravan owners have lovely views across the lagoon. Although separated from the sea, saltwater seeps through the shingle; the water here is brackish and has about half the salt content of sea water. The lagoon marks the location of an old harbour mouth that was in use in the late 1800s and it was formed when the movement of the shingle spits sealed this outlet to the sea.

Saline lagoons are a unique habitat. Much of their biological interest is hidden underwater and specialist invertebrates and plants, that can tolerate the brackish conditions, can survive here. This in turn attracts a wealth of birdlife and during the winter when storms rage at sea, wildfowl can take refuge on the lagoon. During the winter the lagoon is visited by ducks from the far north such as red-breasted merganser and goldeneye. During the summer the reeds attract iridescent dragonflies and damselflies. The dense reedbed provides shelter for many animals; swans nest here, reed and sedge warblers sing from the reeds and the secretive water rail may be heard calling at dawn and dusk – a sound likened to the cries of an animal in mortal agony.

Pagham Lagoon.

Although Pagham Harbour is one big harbour covering an area of over 600 hectares one can regard it as being made up of two halves with different characteristics. The Reserve can be accessed from Selsey and Pagham and as you will see from the two associated walks, they are different. Throughout the Reserve there are well placed information boards that are worth reading as they refer to the area where you are standing at the time.

The lagoon is a haven for birdlife.

The Selsey area is very much dedicated to birdwatchers and has a Visitor Centre by the car park, Discovery Zone and Ferry Hide which is a popular bird hide that overlooks Ferry Pool. Until the eighteenth century Selsey was on an island cut off from the mainland and its name came from the Saxon name of 'Seals-ey' or Island of Seals. Occasionally, seals can still be seen in the sea or resting on the islands. The road between Ferry Channel and Ferry Pool was a crossing point, a ford known as the 'Wadeway' (and The Ferry) but at high tide it had to be crossed by ferry-boat. In 1672 the toll was 'man and horse two pence, foot passengers half a penny'. The present raised causeway which carries the road was built in 1932.

On 27 August 1897 the 'Selsey Tram', officially known as the Hundred of Manhood and Selsey Tramway, began operating between Selsey and Chichester. It was engineered by Colonel Stephens and had eleven 'halts' or stations; troles remain of the crumbling buttresses of the bridge that carried the railway across the Ferry Channel. There is a section of the historic tramway known as The Hedgerow Railway that ran between Ferry and Sidlesham stations. The total construction time took four months and cost £21,570 including land purchase, plus a further £3268 for the engines and carriages. It ran like a railway, but as it operated as a tram company it reduced red tape, including some safety standards. They often laid flat bottomed rails on sleepers directly on to the undulating bare ground. The resulting ride was described as 'the noisiest and most rickety railway in England' and nicknames for the railway included 'The Clickity Click', 'The Bumpety Bump' and 'The Selsey Bumper'.

There was another nickname the 'Hedgerow Railway' due to the fact it hugged the edges of the fields. Bends were often so tight that speeds of over 15mph were impossible. Impromptu farm stops were common to pick up parcels or produce for market and both staff and passengers used to pick blackberries. The tram operated between 1897 and 1935 taking passengers between Selsey and Chichester. It was so slow that the Edwardian cartoonist Cynicus, produced a number of postcards making fun of the railway. In the late 1920s a folk group also composed a song about the railway called 'The Sidlesham Snail'. The lyrics were:

If you live in Sidlesham and do not keep a car,
And you want to go to Chichester the journey isn't far;
The journey is quite simple, the miles they are but few,
If you leave at ten o'clock, you may get there by two.

Chorus:
The Sidlesham snail, the Sidlesham snail,
The boilers burst, she's off the rail.

The Selsey Tram Way footpath marker.

Swans enjoy the Nature Reserve.

Sidlesham Quay.

Crab & Lobster pub.

The 'Selsey Tram' would stop at Sidlesham Station and in its heyday before WWI, the railway carried 80,000 passengers a year. In the 1920s petrol-engine railbuses joined the fleet of ailing trains and gradually took over from the steam engines. The railbuses were more reliable and economical, but they were very noisy and became filled with exhaust fumes. Eventually the advent of the internal combustion engine finally meant the end for the trams. The tram struggled to compete with the local bus service and the increasing popularity of the car. 'The Selsey Tram' ceased operating in 1935 after just thirty-eight years of service. Along certain footpaths in this area there are footpath markers for: The Selsey Tram Way – Hundred of Manhood and Selsey Tramway Co. Ltd. 1896-1935.

A tidal mill once stood at Sidlesham Quay but all that remains today are low brick walls and remnants of the mill pond which can be seen on the other side of the lane. The pond was filled each day by the rising sea and as the sea receded, the water flowing out of the pond powered the mill's machinery. A number of mills were built here from the Middle Ages the last one being built in 1755. The building was left high-and-dry when the harbour was sealed and reclaimed for agriculture in the 1870s. The mill was pulled down and the bricks re-used by a local contractor during WWI. In 1910, during a violent storm, the sea broke through and flooded the area and once again the harbour became intertidal. At low tide a deep channel once navigated by barges, can be seen meandering to the harbour mouth. Sheltered by the shingle spits, tidal waters flow gently and fine sediments are deposited; the saltmarsh that is naturally developing in this flat inlet and the muddy creeks are a refuge for wildlife.

The Crab & Lobster pub at Sidlesham Quay is very popular and is situated beside the harbour with lovely views; it is visited on Walk 9.

The Pagham area around the North Wall is more open with expansive views. The large sluice that is crossed to access the North Wall was built in 2003 as part of a flood relief scheme for the Chichester area. The area of open water and reedbed is known as Breach Pool. The salty water is home to specialist animals and plants that provide a rich food source for migrant and resident birds. The thatched building is known as the Salthouse; its age and original use are unknown though the Pagham Harbour Enclosure Plan of 1974 shows a building in this position. Over the years it has been used as a Rivers Authority tool store and a Home Guard command post; it is now a seasonal information centre. Pagham Harbour Nature Reserve is free to enter but donations to help maintain these facilities are welcome.

Church of St Thomas á Becket.

The local church in Pagham is that of St Thomas á Becket. The first church on this site was built by the Saxons in the seventh century on land given by Caedulla, King of Wessex to St Wilfrid, in gratitude for having saved the people of the area from starvation. Later, when St Wilfrid returned north, he gave Pagham to the Archbishops of Canterbury, who remain Patrons of the parish to this day. The foundations of this early church were rediscovered in 1976. When the church floor was re-laid, some stones from these foundations were built into an oak-topped table which can be seen in the south transept; a piece of Saxon cross was found at the same time. In the 1950s fragments of a Saxon burial urn were found in the churchyard; this was restored by the British Museum and is displayed in a case in the south aisle. After 1066, many new 'lords of the manor' built churches in the Norman style. Pagham was no different and a new larger Norman church was built on the site of the old Saxon one. The font bowl dates from this time and is carved with Norman arches and has a leaf pattern. Archbishop Thomas Becket was murdered in Canterbury Cathedral on 29 December 1170; the church was once again rebuilt within forty years of this date and there is no doubt that this church is one of the earliest to be dedicated to Thomas á Becket.

Saxon urn in St Thomas á Becket church.

Font with Norman arches and leaf pattern

Now you have two walks that you can do around Pagham Harbour. I will see you in the next chapter which takes us to Apuldram by the final short part of Chichester Harbour before exploring the historic city of Chichester.

SUGGESTED WALK

WALK 8. Pagham RSPB Nature Reserve (2.0 miles 3.2 km)

Parking. There is free parking at the RSPB Nature reserve. (Post code PO20 7NE.) Travelling south down the B2145 towards Selsey the Nature Reserve is clearly signed on the left. If you go over the causeway with Ferry Pool on your right and you reach a sharp left bend signed as Upper Norton you have gone 200 yards too far. This is a short, flat and very easy but enjoyable walk with so much to see in a short distance. There are numerous viewing benches between the start and Sidlesham and no stiles. Refreshments are available from the Visitor Centre and the Crab & Lobster pub.

1. From the parking area go through the wide wooden gate that is between the car and coach parking areas – with the road over to your right. Go ahead through a gate signed as Discovery Zone and go over to the right to see tree carvings, a covered seating area and a Dipping pond. On the other side of the pond follow the path as it curves to the right and go through a swing gate. Continue ahead to reach Ferry Hide which overlooks Ferry Pool. This is very popular with bird watchers; the hide was built in 2018 along with the three bug hotels on the outside walls. After visiting the hide continue along the path for a short distance to reach a 3-way footpath sign, signed to Sidlesham Quay 0.8 miles.

Visitor Centre.

Ferry Pool.

Ferry Hide.

Left: Wood carving.

2. Go left with Ferry Channel on your right passing information boards and viewing benches as you go. Just follow this path ignoring any side paths and at the end your reach Mill Lane (not signed) at Sidlesham Quay. Go right along the lane, follow it around to the right and then to the left to arrive at the very popular Crab & Lobster pub.

Typical harbourside paths.

3. After visiting the Crab & Lobster return back to Sidlesham Quay and go back up the lane. Ignore the first footpath on the left that you just arrived from and continue up the lane for a short distance until it bends to the right. At the bend go left by Island Cottage, there is also a footpath sign on the right-hand side of the road showing it is the way to the Visitor Centre. Go along the gravel access road and in a few yards, when the track goes to the right, you continue directly ahead through a swing gate.

Approaching Sidlesham Quay.

Cross this watercourse on the return journey.

Go ahead along a grassy path, back on the Discovery Trail. Just follow this field edge path with trees on your right. In the far corner go through a swing gate and continue ahead along a path through trees. At the end go right by a footpath sign showing to Visitor Centre. In 10 yards go left to another footpath sign and turn right. Follow this path and in a short distance you arrive back at the Visitor Centre.

SUGGESTED WALK

WALK 9. Pagham Harbour Nature Reserve (3.75 miles 6.00 km)

Parking. There is roadside parking in Church Lane just up from the church on the right hand side. (Post code PO21 4NU.) This walk is almost completely level and there is only one stile but there are three fields which can flood after prolonged rain so you will have to be creative with the route you take across one field in particular. There is a lot to see on this walk especially if you are a bird watcher. There are no places for refreshments on this walk.

1. Starting at St Thomas à Becket church go back up the lane to the parking area to reach Grey Barn on your left and turn right past a metal gate into Pagham Harbour Nature Reserve. Follow the path which bends to the left and soon you pass the thatched Information Centre, known as the Salthouse, and in a few more yards you reach the access to the North Wall via a sluice.

2. Go through a swing gate and ahead along Pagham Wall with Pagham Harbour on your left keeping a look out for the varied birdlife, on your right is Breach Pool and further away to the right are views

Thatched Salthouse Visitor Centre.   Pagham Harbour Nature Reserve.

St Thomas à Becket church.

Pagham Harbour sluice gate constructed in 2003.

of the South Downs in the distance. Pass a 3-way footpath sign by some steps (this is where you arrive back on your return journey) and continue along the wall. At the next 3-way footpath sign, where you enter trees, continue left and at the next 3-way footpath sign go right through a metal swing gate. Go ahead along the left edge of a field which can get very wet and muddy and in the far corner continue ahead along the left edge of the next field, which can also be wet

Return path back to the North Wall.

and muddy. Go through a swing gate in the far-left corner and continue ahead along an enclosed path to reach a stile by a 3-way footpath sign.

3. Cross the stile and go immediately right between a wall and a hedgerow. Go through a wooden gate beside a 2-way footpath sign on the left (it can be overgrown) and ahead along the left edge of a field. Cross a concrete bridge and go through a swing gate. (Take note – this next field can get partially flooded with the water being a few inches deep in places. You may have to be creative in the route you take and it may mean detouring over to the right and doubling back on yourself dodging the flooded areas. Have fun and good luck.)

Keep a lookout for the varied birdlife.

Go ahead up the left side of the field on a defined grassy path. Before the end of the field the path arrives at a metal gate on the left with a footpath sign on the left partially hidden in the hedgerow. Go through the metal gate, then immediately turn right up the field with the trees on your right. In the far corner, just before a sleeper bridge, go left across the field on a wide grassy path soon walking with trees beside you on the right. In the far corner, go right at a 3-way footpath sign. Go down a wide track and through a metal gate then ahead along the left edge of a field. Go through a wide metal gate and continue ahead passing a building on your left to reach a metal gate in front of you.

Go through the metal gate and turn immediately right along a right field edge aiming for Pagham Wall ahead. As you walk across this field you will see a footpath sign in the middle on the horizon so just head towards it. Cross a sleeper bridge and go-ahead up steps to reach the footpath sign back on Pagham Wall.

Go left along Pagham Wall and re-pass the Information Centre. Continue ahead following the wide path, past a metal gate, to reach Church Lane. Go left down the lane back to the start.

CHAPTER 8

APULDRAM & CHICHESTER

Chichester Harbour – Fishbourne Channel.

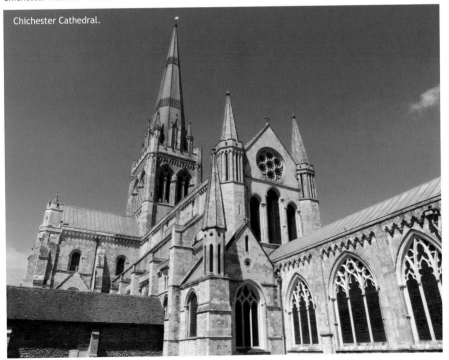

Chichester Cathedral.

APULDRAM

Apuldram (Appledram) is a small village about 2 miles (3km) south-west from the centre of Chichester. Much of the parish is farmland and the village is roughly bounded by the River Lavant to the north, the harbour to the west and by Chichester Marina and Chichester Canal to the south. All that remains of the medieval village is the church, the manor and Rymans – a private manor house built c1410 and only open to the public on special occasions. Apuldram contains the old port of Dell Quay which is now only used by smaller cabin cruisers and yachts but it used to be a fairly large port that served Chichester. The silting up of the northern reaches of Chichester Harbour made Dell Quay uncommercial and Dell Quay is best known today for the sixteenth-century Crown and Anchor pub which sits enjoying views overlooking the Fishbourne Channel of Chichester Harbour. Try to imagine as you sit there enjoying your drink that in Roman times the harbour was navigable all the way to Fishbourne and Roman galleys may have sailed right past you to Fishbourne Palace.

There are various birds to be seen by Fishbourne Channel.

Fishbourne Channel – Chichester Harbour.

The meaning of the name Apuldram is as picturesque as its setting. It is made up of two Old English words apulder (apple) and ham(m) (an enclosure). W. D. Peckham a local historian once quoted in *The Place-Names of Sussex* Part I 1929 – the deep loam with a clay or brick-earth subsoil, is admirable apple-growing land to this day.

In Saxon times and for a time after the Norman Conquest, Apuldram was part of the Manor of Bosham, which in the eleventh century, during the reign of Edward the Confessor, belonged to Godwin, the powerful Earl of Wessex, whose son Harold was defeated at the Battle of Hastings. After the Conquest William I took possession of the Manor. In 1125 Henry I gave the parish to the Abbot of Brethren of Battle Abbey but the College of Bosham remained responsible for ecclesiastical matters and one of the six canons of the College held the Prebend (the portion of the revenues of a cathedral or collegiate church formerly granted to a canon or member of the chapter as his stipend) and paid a deputy to live in and care for the parish. The Prebend of Apuldram was once held by William of Wykeham, Bishop of Winchester. In 1197 Battle granted possession to Sir Michael de Appeltrieham, the Sheriff of Sussex. The demesne reverted to the Crown following the Dissolution of the Monasteries between 1538 and 1542 and in 1580 Elizabeth I granted it to William, Baron Howard of Effingham. Upon his death it passed to his son Charles who was Lord High Admiral from 1585 to 1618 and who commanded the fleet that defeated the Spanish Armada.

Church of St Mary the Virgin.

The church of St Mary the Virgin, which stands at the northern end of this rectangular parish, is thought to have been built c1100 but the main building was built in its present form c1250, and the south aisle was added to the nave about one hundred years later. A south porch was built in the fifteenth century and a vestry and heating chamber were erected on the north side of the nave in the nineteenth century. The chancel is an example of thirteenth century architecture with three great lancet windows with Purbeck marble shafts and stone mouldings.

CHICHESTER

Chichester (Noviomagus Reginorum in Roman times) is a cathedral city and the only city in West Sussex. It is one of the great well-preserved Georgian cities in the UK and has played a key role of the affairs of Sussex since at least Roman times. Today it is the prosperous administrative capital of West Sussex and it is the seat of the Church of England Diocese of Chichester, with a twelfth-century cathedral. The city streets are packed with listed buildings and the pedestrianised city centre is enclosed within ancient city walls. The area around Chichester is believed to have been significant during the Roman invasion of 43 AD, as confirmed by evidence of military storage structures near Fishbourne Roman Palace. The city centre is on the foundations of the Romano-British city of Noviomagus Reginorum, capital of the Civitas Reginorum. Stane Street is a Roman road that connects the city with London, and started at the east gate, while the Chichester to Silchester road started from the north gate. The city plan comes from the Romans – the North, South, East and West shopping streets radiate from the central Market Cross which dates from medieval times. The original Roman city wall was over 2 metres (6.5ft) thick with a steep ditch. It survived for over one thousand five hundred years and was replaced by a thinner Georgian wall. The city was also home to a Roman baths which were found during preparation works for a new car park and are now displayed in the Novium Museum. Just outside the city walls an amphitheatre was built close to east gate in around 80 AD.

Chichester Cathedral is steeped in history, is an architectural delight and contains many works of art and stained-glass windows. A monastery was founded in 681 by St Wilfrid near the coast in Selsey and it became the first cathedral in

Remains of Roman Baths on display at the Novium Museum.

Sussex. Following the Norman Conquest of 1066, the Council of London deemed that cathedrals that were located in remote locations should be moved to more populous areas; so, in 1076 the See of Chichester was established and the bishopric moved to the old Roman city of Chichester. Using stone from Quarr on the Isle of Wight, construction began in 1076 on a new cathedral, overseen by Stigand, the first Norman bishop. Chichester Cathedral was eventually completed by Bishop Ralph Luffa and consecrated in 1108.

A series of fires in 1114 and 1187 saw the destruction of the cathedral's wooden roof and eastern end; in its place, Bishop Seffrid II built a stone-vaulted roof and remodelled much of the building. The cathedral was then re-consecrated in 1199. An important figure in the cathedral's history is Richard of Wych, bishop of Chichester from 1245–1253, who was canonized by Pope Urban in 1262 for his holy works and miracles. In 1276, when Richard's body was moved (translated) from its first burial place in the chapel of St Thomas and St Edmund to the Retroquire (the space behind the high altar in a church or cathedral) the service grew great crowds, including the new king, Edward I.

Around c1400 the cathedral's spire, cloisters and Bell Tower were built and Chichester is unique in having the only surviving detached medieval bell tower, situated by the cathedral's western end. St Richard's shrine continued to attract dedicated pilgrims until it was destroyed in 1538 during the violent turmoil of the Reformation.

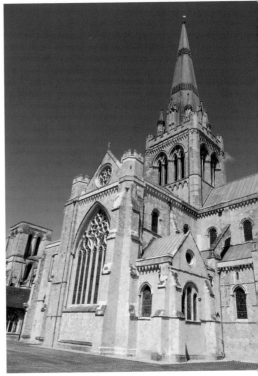

Chichester Cathedral.

St Richard – Chichester's patron saint.

Since the nineteenth century, depictions of St. Richard have returned to the cathedral and in 1930 an altar was restored to the original site of his shrine. Almost 800 years after his death, St Richard of Chichester is patron saint of Sussex and his saint's day of 16 June is celebrated as Sussex Day.

The outbreak of the English Civil War in 1642 saw Parliamentary forces take control of the city, ransacking Chichester Cathedral in the process. It took until after the Restoration of the monarchy in 1660 for a programme of restoration to be instigated to undo the damage done.

Serious cracks appeared in the masonry and the cathedral's tower and spire collapsed in 1861. A programme of rebuilding overseen by Sir George Gilbert Scott took over five years before both were repaired and the cathedral was able to fully reopen for worship in 1866. The twentieth century saw the cathedral move into the world of modern art with the commissioning of pieces by respected artists such as Graham Sutherland, John Piper and Marc Chagall which are on permanent display. The cathedral is open daily and is free to visit but it does rely on donations.

Market Cross (Chichester Cross) is a perpendicular market cross in the centre of Chichester at the intersection of North, East, South and West Streets in view of Chichester Cathedral; it is a Grade 1 listed building. From an inscription on it, the cross was built by Edward Story, Bishop of Chichester from 1477 to 1503 and the cross is believed

Market Cross (Chichester Cross).

to have been built in 1501 after Bishop Edward Story paid ten pounds to the Mayor of Chichester for the ground on which it is built. Over the years the cross has become a popular landmark in Chichester. The Market Cross is built of Caen stone which was the most favoured building stone of the time. It is octagonal with a strong butment at each angle, surmounted with pinnacles. There is an entrance on each of its sides through a pointed arch, ornamented with crockets and a finial. Above this on all four sides is a clock showing the time to the people walking down the main streets. In the centre is a large circular column, the basement forming a seat: into this column is inserted a number of groinings which, spreading from the centre, form a moulded roof.

The Novium Museum first opened its doors to the public on 8 July 2012. Located in Tower Street the Novium is purpose-built to show the remains of a Roman bath house which were uncovered during preparation works for a new car park. The building was designed by Keith Williams Architects whose other projects include the Wexford Opera House in Ireland and The Unicorn Theatre in London. The Museum also displays the Bosham Head (Chapter 3). The Museum is free to enter but does rely on donations.

Now you can do the associated walk around the historic city of Chichester and visit the stunning Chichester Cathedral. Don't forget to visit the Novium Museum to see the remains of the Roman baths but also the Bosham Head that was featured in Chapter 3. I will see you in Chapter 9 where we will explore Royal Bognor Regis.

Market Cross (Chichester Cross).

73

SUGGESTED WALK

WALK 10. Fishbourne Channel, Chichester Cathedral and Market Cross
(6.0 miles 9.7 km)

Parking. There is a small car park in Church Lane by Apuldram Church. Church Lane is on a sharp bend off Appledram Lane South but the church is signposted – avoid doing this walk on a Sunday as the car park is small. (Post code PO20 7EG.) This is an easy level walk across fields and through the centre of Chichester, there is one stile. There is plenty to see on this walk starting with the final part of Chichester Harbour – the Fishbourne Channel. We also visit St Mary the Virgin church at Apuldram as well as the historic city of Chichester before heading back along a similar route. There are many bars, restaurants and shops in Chichester for refreshments.

1. From the car park, go along the path beside the church notice board to reach St Mary the Virgin church. Just before the church, go left out of the churchyard and continue along the left edge of a field; over to your right you get your first view of Chichester Cathedral in the distance as well as the not so picturesque sewage works somewhat closer to you. In the field corner, go through a swing gate and go ahead to reach Fishbourne Channel by a 3-way footpath sign – this is the final part of your walk around Chichester Harbour from Chapters 1–4.

St Mary the Virgin church.

Fishbourne Channel.

2. Turn right and walk with the channel on your left. At a 3-way footpath sign, go through a swing gate and continue beside the channel keeping a look out for the varied birdlife. At the next 3-way footpath sign, don't go through the swing gate but continue beside the channel on a slightly raised bank. Soon the bank curves to the right and you have another view of Chichester Cathedral directly ahead. Cross a small bridge to reach a 3-way footpath sign. Go left and in a few yards the path curves to the right. Cross a sleeper bridge and continue with a

barbed-wire fence on your left at first and then proceed along a path aiming for buildings ahead. Cross another sleeper bridge, ignoring the swing gate on the right. Continue ahead and go through a swing gate then cross a substantial bridge. Go ahead along sleeper boards and in 20 yards go right and cross another bridge. Follow the left edge of a field with a crystal-clear stream beside you.

Go ahead along more sleeper boards to reach a 2-way footpath sign by a swing gate. Go left and follow a right field edge then go diagonally right across the field aiming for the far-left corner to the left of a wooden building. (Ignore the substantial 4-way footpath sign on the left). Go through a swing gate and ahead to the left of the building to a 2-way footpath sign via a stile. Follow the access drive out to the main A259.

3. Go left along the road and in about 50 yards cross over via an island and continue along the road. In 25 yards go right and through the underpass beneath the A27 then continue ahead along Fishbourne Road, not signed. Just follow the road and when you reach a green bridge over the railway, cross it using the steps on both sides of the railway and being wary of cyclists who also use this bridge. On the far side, go right with a school on the left.

Follow the concrete path (Centurion Way) and in a few yards you reach a mini roundabout. Continue ahead along Westgate, not named but signed to the City Centre, with the school playing field on your left behind the hedgerow. At a mini roundabout continue ahead along Westgate. Just keep going and at the end you reach a roundabout. Continue ahead at the roundabout along West Street and soon you reach the magnificent Chichester Cathedral on the right – when you

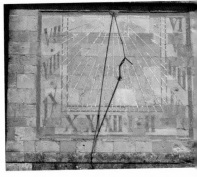

Look for the smaller details including a sundial and humorous gargoyles.

wander around the cathedral make sure you look for the smaller details like the sundials and the almost humorous gargoyles. (On the left opposite the cathedral is the former church of Peter the Great which is now a bar and a few yards along Tower Street, beside the former church, is the Novium Museum on the right with the remains of the Roman baths and the Bosham Head.)

Old church of Peter the Great – now a bar.

Just a few examples of the beauty of
Chichester Cathedral.

4. After visiting the cathedral, continue along West Street and in a few yards, you reach Market Cross which is regularly referred to as a clock tower – again look out for the smaller details on this building. (If you want to go and explore Chichester use this as your return point.)

Market Cross with its smaller, often overlooked, details.

Turn right down South Street, passing Canon's Gate on the right, and near the end when you reach the Fountain pub on the right turn right along Southgate which is beside the pub. Walk through to reach a small car park and go left through the car park to reach the height restriction barrier at its entrance. At the height restriction, go right and follow the path along Walls Walk with a

Canon's Gate.

View from Walls Walk.

stream (possibly dry) and cathedral on your right.

Just follow the path to reach a road at the end. Cross the double road and continue directly ahead along the right edge of a field. At an access road, by a footpath sign, go right over the stream and go ahead along a wide cycle path to arrive back at Westgate, not signed. Turn left along Westgate and just retrace your outward journey, crossing a roundabout, to reach the bridge over the railway at the end of the road. Cross the railway and on the far side, go ahead along the residential Fishbourne Road opposite (not left towards the roundabout by Tesco). At the end of the road, go back under the A27 and at a 3-way footpath sign go left beside the A259. In a few yards cross over via the island, continue for about 50 yards then go right at a footpath sign.

Go back up the access drive and in a few yards go left through the car park to reach the church of St Peter and St Mary. As you approach the church you reach a notice board by a junction of paths; go right along the path to reach a swing gate. Go through the swing gate and go immediately left to another swing gate by a 4-way footpath sign. Go through the swing gate and across a field. On the far side go through a gap in the hedgerow and go almost directly ahead across the field as directed by the footpath sign; this field may have crops growing.

On the far side, go ahead over the stream and in 10 yards go left through a swing gate and continue along a left field edge. On the far side go through a swing gate and go left back beside the Fishbourne Channel. Follow the channel, go

through a swing gate and ahead along the right edge of a field at first then go diagonally left up to a swing gate in the far-left corner of the field. Go through the gate and up the right edge of the field aiming for the church ahead. Pass to the right of the church then turn right down the access path back to the start.

Church of St Peter and St Mary.

CHAPTER 9
ALDWICK, ROYAL BOGNOR REGIS & FELPHAM

Insert: Bognor Regis beach looking east towards Felpham.

Royal Bognor Regis Pier.

ROYAL BOGNOR REGIS

Royal Bognor Regis is a seaside town and popular holiday resort; it is a very built-up area and includes the nearby coastal villages of Aldwick and Felpham which are now suburbs of Bognor Regis. Bognor is one of the oldest recorded Anglo-Saxon place names in Sussex and in a document of 680 it is referred to as Bucgan ora meaning Bucge's (a female Anglo-Saxon name) shore, or landing place. Originally it was named just Bognor and was a fishing and smuggling village until the eighteenth century when it was converted into a resort by Sir Richard Hotham who renamed the settlement Hothampton, which didn't catch on. Bognor was originally part of the ancient parish of Pagham with a port or haven on the Aldingbourne rife.

It has been suggested that Hotham and his new resort are portrayed in Jane Austen's unfinished novel *Sanditon*. The resort grew slowly in the first half of the nineteenth century but grew quickly following the coming of the railway in 1864. It was in 1929 that the area was chosen by advisors to King George V which led to its regal suffix, by royal consent.

King George V became ill and required lung surgery to be carried out on 12 December 1928. His recovery was slow and on 22 January 1929 Buckingham Palace issued the statement saying 'It had been realised by the King's medical advisors that, prior to the establishment of convalescence, there would arrive a time when sea air would be necessary in order to secure the continuation of His Majesty's progress.' The statement continued 'with the knowledge, a careful search was made for a "residence" not only suitable in itself but possessing the necessary attributes of close proximity to the sea, southern exposure, protection from wind, privacy and reasonable access to and from London.'

Bognor beach is shingle with sand when the tide is out.

The residence chosen was Craigweil House (demolished in 1939) which was placed at His Majesty's disposal by owner Sir Arthur Du Cros who was a wealthy businessman, having acquired the house from Dr Stocker who brought it from the Countess of Newburgh who had constructed the building in 1806; the house was actually in Aldwick. As a result of this the king was asked to bestow the suffix 'Regis' (of the King) on Bognor. The petition requesting this was presented to Lord Stamfordham, who was the King's Private Secretary, who then delivered it to the King. King George supposedly replied, 'Oh Bugger Bognor'. Lord Stamfordham then went back to the petitioners and told them that 'the King has been graciously pleased to grant your request.' There is also a slightly different version of the 'Bugger Bogner' story in that the King, upon being told, shortly before his death, that he would soon be well enough to revisit the town, uttered those words. There is little evidence to confirm that these words were actually spoken in this context but although the sea air did help the King regain his health, it is certain that the King had little regard for the town.

Today Bognor is very well-known for Butlin's which has been present in the town since the early 1930s when an amusement park and zoo were opened. A holiday camp opened in 1960 and this has recently moved towards hotel accommodation with modern amenities.

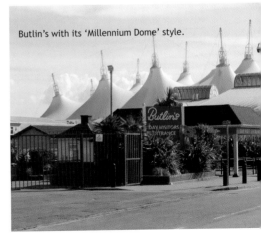

Butlin's with its 'Millennium Dome' style.

On the beach between Bognor Regis and Aldwick there is the wreck of a floating pontoon (caisson) which was part of the Mulberry floating harbours used by the Allies to invade the French coast on D-Day 6 June 1944. It formed part of the Mulberry harbour which broke free in a storm on 4 June, the day before it was due to go over the channel to Arromanche. This section of Mulberry was abandoned and did not make it across the Channel, instead it washed up on the beach shortly after D-Day and is still visible at low tide throughout the year.

Mulberry floating harbour (pontoon) Aldwick.

Bognor Regis still has several areas and buildings that link it to its past including the Royal Norfolk Hotel and Hotham Park. The Royal Norfolk beachfront hotel was built in 1830 in the classic Regency style and has an imposing façade with views across the English Channel.

Sir Richard Hotham built Hotham Park House in 1792. It was in 1787 that he laid the first foundation stone of his new seaside resort thereby becoming

Hotham Park House.

the founder of Bognor. He only lived here for seven years before his death in 1799. At that time his mansion was named The Lodge and it had its own private chapel. The clock tower is the only remaining part of the chapel which still houses Hotham's clock from 1794 made by John Thwaites of Clerkenwell. Sir Richard Hotham died on 13 March 1799, eighteen months before William Blake's arrival in Felpham. He was buried in the parish church of St Mary Magdalene at South Bersted. His grave can still be seen today and an annual wreath laying ceremony celebrates his contribution to the community and the fact that, as with William

Hotham Park wood carving – one of several to look out for.

Blake, one person's vision can live on through future generations.

Hotham Park covers an area of 22 acres (9 hectares) and is located in the High Street near Butlins. It first became a public park on 1st January 1947 having been purchased by the former Bognor Regis Urban District Council from the executors of the late William Fletcher. Locally the park is the most important heritage amenity in Bognor Regis and the house built by Sir Richard Hotham remains intact. The grounds have eroded since 1947 and only the walled parkland and nearby Millberry Wood remains open to the public. The horticultural interest in the park was chiefly created by William Fletcher between 1900 and 1940. Most of the shrub and herb layers were destroyed in a hurricane in 1987, but the remnants of a fine tree collection still remain. In 1977 Abraham Singer purchased the house; he was keen on its history and decided to restore it inside and out, whilst retaining the charm, character and features of the building. The building was divided into several apartments that are privately occupied to this day.

Bognor Regis Pier and HMS *St Barbara* memorial plaque.

The first structure of Bognor Pier began in 1864 and was completed by May 1865 at a cost of £5000. A kiosk was built at the shore end and a charge of one old penny (1d) was charged to allow the public to walk the length of the pier. It was sold to what was to become Bognor Urban District Council in 1876 for £1200. The new owners added a bandstand and in July 1900 a pavilion was added part-way down the pier. In 1901 a landing stage allowed for paddle steamers to tie up at the pier but this was short lived and in 1906 it became redundant as ships grew too large. Ongoing repairs and maintenance became a problem for the council and the pier was sold on to private investors for 10s 6d. The pavilion was closed for major restoration work and was re-opened in 1909. Over the coming years, Bognor Regis's first cinema was added to the shore end of the pier, as well as a theatre, roof garden restaurant and a few shops.

In 1936 a three-tier landing stage was erected and catered for paddle steamers and smaller boats. Diving displays became a regular spectacle throughout the summer season. During WWII Bognor Regis pier was renamed HMS *St Barbara* as it was given the role of observation station for the Royal Navy. One claim to fame was on the 10 February 1943 the piers guns shot down a German Dornier D0217 bomber aircraft which had strayed within their sights. In 2017 a new memorial dedicated to HMS *St Barbara* was unveiled at the front of Bognor Regis pier.

Between 1964 and 1967 severe storms caused part of the structure to collapse and the pavilion was lost. The pier was sold to an American company who closed it in December 1974 due to severe fire damage on two occasions. In 1989 the pier was awarded Grade II listed status by English Heritage but in 1994 it was in such decline that an application was made to demolish part of the structure. Bognor Pier Leisure Ltd stepped in but being unable to secure a grant to restore it nothing more happened. Severe storms in 1999 caused more damage and another part of the pier was lost. The bad weather of recent years has weakened it further and the end of the pier has been removed for safety reasons leaving it a fraction of what it once was.

The International Bognor Birdman was an annual competition for human-powered 'flying' machines that was held each summer on Bognor pier. The contestants launched themselves from the end of the pier and a prize was awarded to the one that glided the furthest distance. The competition was rarely taken seriously and the event gave the competitors a chance to construct and fly improbable machines whilst wearing an outlandish costume. The competition attracted a sizable crowd as well as the local media and competitors to have taken part include Sir Richard Branson.

ALDWICK

Aldwick is a seaside area between Pagham and Bognor Regis and is one of the more genteel parts of Bognor Regis. Now that Bognor Regis has spread its way all along the coast swamping all the old seaside villages from Elmer in the east to Pagham Harbour in the west, Aldwick has lost a little of its identity. The beach is the same as Bognor Regis and Felpham in that it has shingle at the top with exposed sand once the tide goes out. Along the top of the beach are some quite colourful beach huts which adds to its charm.

Aldwick was briefly a home of King George V when he convalesced here at Craigweil House in 1929, before its demolition and the King's wider family would regularly visit him. This led directly to Bognor attaining the suffix 'Regis' and it was after this that Aldwick became a haven for rich seasiders. South of Aldwick, beneath the waves, are the remains of the lost hamlet of Charlton which was slowly overcome by rising sea levels in the sixteenth century when the villagers were forced to leave. As already mentioned on the beach between Bognor Regis and Aldwick there is the wreck of a floating pontoon (caisson) which was part of the Mulberry floating harbours used by the Allies to invade the French coast on D-Day 6 June 1944.

Aldwick beach towards Pagham.   Insert: Mulberry floating harbour.

FELPHAM

Felpham is the next village to the east of Bognor Regis. The beach is the same as the beach at Bognor with shingle at the top and great expanses of sand when the tide is out. Bognor promenade continues into Felpham before continuing as a footpath towards Middleton-on Sea.

Felpham beach towards Bognor Regis.

Felpham beach towards Middleton-on-Sea.

Felpham existed long before Bognor Regis and was mentioned in the Domesday Book under the hundred of Binstead. The poet William Blake, who was introduced to the village by his friend William Hayley, lived in Felpham for three years while writing his *Milton: A Poem in Two Books*. The poem contains the words about 'England's green and pleasant land', today known as the anthem 'Jerusalem', which were inspired by Blake's 'evident pleasure' in the Felpham countryside. The cottage where Blake lived is depicted in the illustrations for the poem. Of the village he wrote:

William Blake's Cottage.

WILLIAM BLAKE
Artist, Poet & Mystic,
Lived here 1800-1803

> Away to sweet Felpham for
> heaven is there:
> The Ladder of Angels
> descends through the air
>
> On the turret its spiral does
> softly descend
>
> Through the village it winds,
> at my cot it does end.

The 'turret' refers to Hayley's house, east of the church, which he built around 1800. It was Hayley who was also famous in his day for turning down the offer of the position of Poet Laureate in 1790. William Blake also experienced the restorative power of the sea and in a letter he sent to Thomas Butts in 1800, Blake recounts his joy at observing nature from the sands of Felpham beach:

To my Friend Butts I write
My first Vision of Light,
On the yellow sands sitting.
The Sun was emitting
His glorious beams
From Heaven's high streams.

St Mary's church.

Blake has a road named after him, Blake's Road, on which his former residence is still sited. The cottage is one of only two remaining properties that William Blake lived in. Blake and his wife moved here in in 1800 and he considered the village to be idyllic and wrote to his friend, Mrs Anna Flaxman that:

'The bread of sweet thought
And the wine of delight
Feed the village of Felpham
By day and by night.'

It was at this time that that England was on high alert due to Napoleon taking control of France following the French Revolution. A peace treaty made between Britain and France in

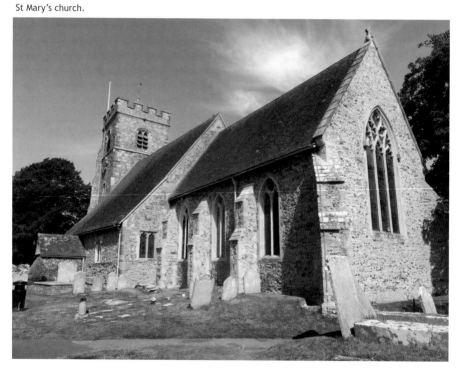

1802 was soon broken by the French and British soldiers were stationed at intervals all along the south coast, including Felpham, in case of an invasion from the Revolutionaries. One such man was Private John Scofield, a soldier with the First Dragoon guards who went into William Blake's garden on 12 August 1803. Both men exchanged words and Blake physically escorted Scofield off his land and towards the Fox Inn. Scofield accused Blake of shouting 'Damn the King' and 'All soldiers are slaves' but he was later acquitted in Chichester.

With his tenancy ending and damp in the cottage affecting his and his wife's health, Blake and his wife returned to London on 18 September 1803. In a letter he had sent to his brother James dated 30 January 1803 he had written 'my wife has agues and rheumatisms almost ever she has been here'. There is a memorial window dedicated to William Blake in St Mary's church, Felpham.

Stained glass memorial window.

Now that we have reached Felpham we are going to take a short break from the coast and I will see you in Chapter 10 at Boxgrove for the first of five walks that take you to local villages that have an association with the coast. We will re-join the coastal journey at Middleton-on-Sea in Chapter 11.

ENGLISH CHANNEL

Whilst walking along the West Sussex coast you are never far from the English Channel. If you follow the book from Thorney Island to Brighton it is on your right-hand side all the way. So, as this is the first chapter in the book that doesn't have an associated walk, I thought I would take this opportunity to give you some facts and figures about it.

The English Channel, also known as the Channel, is considered by many people to be the stretch of water that separates the south of England from northern France and that to get between the two you go by ferry or the Channel Tunnel; it is, of course, much more than this. The English Channel (from here referred to as the Channel) is an arm of the Atlantic Ocean that links to the southern part of the North Sea by the Strait of Dover at its north-eastern end and it is the busiest shipping area in the world.

It is approximately 350 miles long (560 km) and its width varies from 150 miles (240 km) to 21 miles (34 km) in the Strait of Dover in Kent and covers an area of 29,000 sq. miles (75,000 sq. km). The Strait of Dover, at the eastern end is the narrowest point and its widest point is near its midpoint between Lyme Bay and the Gulf of Saint Malo. It is quite shallow with an average depth of 390 ft (120m) at its widest part to 148 ft (45m) between Dover and Calais.

Between the Isle of Wight and the mainland there is a small parallel strait known as the Solent which is 20 miles (32km) long and varies between 2.5 and 5 miles (4 and 8 km) in width. The Solent is a major shipping lane for passenger, freight and military vessels and is an important area for water sports particularly yachting hosting the famous yearly Cowes Week.

Until the eighteenth century the Channel was known colloquially to the English as the 'Narrow Sea' and it was never defined as a political border or considered the property of a nation. The name 'English Channel' has been widely used since the early eighteenth century, possibly originating from the designation 'Engelse Kanaal' on Dutch sea maps from the sixteenth century onwards. The French have used the name La Manche since the seventeenth century; the name is said to refer to the Channel's sleeve shape (la manche is French for sleeve).

There are several major islands in the Channel, the most notable, and in this book most noticeable, is the Isle of Wight which can easily be seen from the Bracklesham and Selsey area. The other main islands are the Channel Islands which are British Crown dependencies off the coast of France.

The Channel acts as a funnel that amplifies the tidal range and in the UK Shipping Forecast the Channel is divided into the following areas, from the east: Dover, Wight, Portland, Plymouth.

The Channel has traffic on both the UK-Europe and North Sea-Atlantic routes, and is the world's busiest seaway with over 500 ships per day. After an accident in January 1971 and a series of collisions with wreckage in the following February, the Dover TSS, the world's first radar-controlled Traffic Separation Scheme, was set up

Rampion Wind Farm through the sea haze.   Inshore lifeboat.

by the International Maritime Organisation. The scheme means that vessels travelling north must use the French side of the Channel and vessels travelling south must use the English side; there is a separation zone between the two lanes. In December 2002 the Norwegian-flagged MV *Tricolor*, that was carrying £30m of luxury cars, sank 20 miles (32 km) northwest of Dunkirk after it collided with the container ship *Kariba* in fog. The cargo ship *Nicola* ran into the wreckage the next day; there was no loss of life.

The shore-based long-range traffic control system was updated in 2003 and there is a series of traffic separation systems in operation. Although the system is unable to reach the levels of safety obtained from aviation systems such as the Traffic Collision Avoidance System (TCAS) it has reduced the number of shipping accidents.

Rampion is an offshore wind farm development by EON, off the Sussex coast. It is located between 8 and 16 miles (13 and 25 km) from the shore and is situated off the coastal towns of Worthing to the west, Brighton in the centre and Seaford to the east. It lies in an irregular elongated area, approximately 17 miles (28 km) in an east to west direction and approximately 6.2 miles (10 km) in a north to south direction, an area of 27.8 sq. miles (72 sq. km).

Commissioned in April 2018, the area has become a local landmark and can be seen from great distances but the jury is out as to whether you love it or hate it. Rampion Offshore Wind Farm is now generating enough green electricity to power the equivalent of around 350,000 UK homes; this is around half of the homes in Sussex. It was in July 2010 that the public voted for the name Rampion following a school's competition. Rampion, is the county flower of Sussex and the name was submitted by Davison High School.

Each year many travellers cross beneath the Channel using the Channel Tunnel. A tunnel was first proposed in the early nineteenth century and the tunnel finally opened in 1994, connecting the UK and France by rail. Today it is a routine journey to travel between Paris or Brussels and London on the Eurostar train. Freight trains also use the tunnel and cars, coaches and lorries are carried on Eurostar Shuttle trains between Folkestone and Calais.

Coastal resorts on both sides of the Channel, such as Brighton and Deauville, started an era of aristocratic tourism in the early nineteenth century, which developed into the seaside tourism that has shaped resorts around the world. Short trips across the Channel for leisure purposes are often referred to as Channel Hopping or, as I know it, Booze Cruise.

CHAPTER 10
BOXGROVE, HALNAKER, SLINDON, TORTINGTON & ARUNDEL

BOXGROVE

Boxgrove is a village about 3.5 miles northeast of Chichester; it is just south of the A285 which follows the line of the Roman road Stane Street. The parish has an area of 1169 hectares (2890 acres) and included in the parish are the hamlets of Crockerhill, Strettington and Halnaker.

Boxgrove is known for the Lower Palaeolithic archaeological site that was discovered in a gravel quarry known as Amey's Eartham Pit located near the village but in Eartham Parish. Parts of the site complex were excavated between 1983 and 1996 by a team from University College London. Numerous Acheulean flint tools and remains of animals, some butchered, dating from around 500,000 years ago were found; showing that this area was used by some of the earliest occupants of the British Isles. Boxgrove is also famous for the discovery of the remains of *Homo Heidelbergensis* (Boxgrove Man) in 1994. It is thought to be 500,000 years old and is the only postcranial hominid bone to have been found in Northern Europe; teeth from another individual were found two years later. The site has been bought by English Heritage so further finds are possible.

In 1622 several parishioners of Boxgrove were prosecuted for playing cricket in the churchyard. There were three reasons for the prosecution: one it contravened a local bye-law, another reflected concern about windows which may or may not have been broken and the third was the charge that 'a little childe had like to have her braines beaten out with a cricket batt'.

Guest House ruins.

The Benedictine priory of St Mary the Virgin and St Blaise was founded around 1117 during the reign of Henry I by Robert de la Haye, Lord of Halnaker; a Saxon church had existed on the site before the Conquest. It was a cell of the abbey at Lessay in Normandy and when founded it only had a community of three Benedictine monks. In about 1126, upon the marriage of Robert's daughter Cecily to Roger St John the number of monks living at Boxgrove was increased to six. Robert had died by 1165 and by 1187 there were 15 monks. In 1339, when other alien monastic properties were seized by Edward III, Boxgrove became independent. Following the Dissolution of the Monasteries the buildings and land were granted to Sir Thomas West, Baron de la Warr.

Of the monastic buildings only the ruins of the Guest House and part of the church and chapter house remain. They are grouped around a small field which is

Boxgrove Priory.

Burial tomb chest of Admiral Philip Nelson-Ward.

the site of the cloister of the monastery. At the northern edge of the site the ruin of the fourteenth-century guest house stands alone; it is roofless but the north and south gable ends still stand to their full height. The building originally had two storeys with an undercroft or vaulted cellar that was used for storage. The support for the vault of the undercroft can be seen at the north end of the building.

The west part of the monastic church was demolished in the eighteenth century but the chancel, central tower, transepts and easternmost bay of the nave survive as the impressive present-day church; there is a model of the monastic buildings inside the church to help understand the layout of the monastery. The north wall of the nave forms part of the wall of the churchyard and the footings of the south wall and one bay of the south arcade from the interior of the church can also be seen in the churchyard. One wall of the chapter house where the monks would have gathered daily to have a chapter of the rule of St Benedict read to them is attached to the north transept of the church; it has a central doorway with a window to either side. The remaining monastery buildings lay to the north of the church surrounding the cloister but do not survive above ground.

Stained glass.

There is so much more that can be written about the Priory particularly about the inside of the building including the stained-glass windows that would require a complete book to do it justice so it is best you visit for yourself where there is more detailed literature available for you to buy.

Now you can do walk 11 around the nearby fields where you will get views of the Priory and Guest House ruins from different angles and I will see you at Halnaker Windmill where there are limited views down to the Priory as well as extensive views along the West Sussex coast and beyond.

Statues and works of art are everywhere.

SUGGESTED WALK

WALK 11. Boxgrove Priory & Ruins (2.5 miles 4.0 km)

Parking. Village Hall car park in The Street. (Post code PO18 0EE.) This walk has been kept deliberately short so that it is easily achievable by all and everyone can appreciate the beauty of the Priory. The walk is across fields and along tracks that are all level and there are no stiles. There are no places for refreshments on this walk.

1. From the car park, go right down the road and in a few yards cross over and go along the gravel access road opposite signposted to Boxgrove Priory. Follow the access road around to the right and soon you reach the Priory ruins on the left and Boxgrove Priory next to the ruins on the right.

Boxgrove Priory.

2. After visiting this area, leave the Priory grounds via the opposite exit which is along the path directly opposite the main door to the Priory. Immediately turn left through a swing gate and head out across the middle of a large field; there is a good view of Halnaker windmill on the hill to your left which you can visit on the other short walk. Go through a gap in the row of trees and immediately go left as directed by a 3-way footpath sign.

De la Warr Chantry Chapel.

Chapel reredos.

Church organ.

Go along the left field edge with a good view of the ruins on your left, and in a short distance, at a junction with two gates on the left and by a 3-way footpath sign, go right up a wide grassy path and walk between a vineyard on the left and a hedgerow on the right. Just follow the path and at a junction, go ahead as directed by a 3-way footpath sign and continue beside a solitary row of trees on your right. At the end of the row of trees, go left through a swing gate; take two paces to the left then follow the wide track ahead. Keep following this track ahead and soon it naturally filters into Tinwood Lane, not signed. Pass a stile on the right and in a few more yards, just as the lane starts to curve to the right, go left up four steps and go through a swing gate by a footpath sign.

3. Go ahead along the wide grassy path with a vineyard on your right and two rows of trees on your left. At the end of the vineyard, continue ahead along a more enclosed path to reach a 3-way footpath sign; go left here and walk beneath power lines. At a 2-way footpath sign, go right and follow the path between trees with fields on either side to reach an access track by a 3-way footpath sign. Go right here and follow the grassy path with hedgerow on your left out to The Street. Cross over, go through the gap in the hedgerow by a footpath sign and go ahead / left straight into the car park back at the start.

Now you can do Walk 11a to visit Halnaker Windmill. It is only a couple of miles away and it is a short 1.75 mile (2.8 km) walk. From the windmill you get a limited view back down to Boxgrove Priory as well as extensive views along the West Sussex coast and beyond.

Priory and Guest House ruins from the walk.

HALNAKER

Halnaker is a hamlet located about 3.5 miles northeast of Chichester along the old Roman road Stane Street and it is best known for its windmill which is popular with both children and adults alike.

In medieval times Halnaker was also referred to as Halfnaked. *Kelly's Directory* of 1867 says that Boxgrove manor-house is said to have been built by Sir Thomas West, who married, early in the reign of Henry VIII, Elizabeth, the heiress of John Bonville, of Halnaker.

To the north of the village, the very popular Halnaker Windmill is a tower mill located at 128 metres (420ft) above sea level on Halnaker Hill. The mill is visible from many miles and the views from the mill are far reaching along the south coast to the Isle of Wight, Portsmouth and the Rampion Wind Farm off Shoreham coast is easily visible. The mill is easily reached by a short walk (Walk 11a). It is well maintained externally but there is no machinery inside the mill and, sadly you cannot go inside the mill as it has been closed off due to regular acts of mindless vandalism. However, that does not spoil the experience of visiting the mill and appreciating the views that the mill proudly enjoys.

The mill was first mentioned in 1540 as belonging to the manor of 'Halfnaked'. It was built for the Duke of Richmond as the feudal mill of the Goodwood Estate.

The surviving mill is believed to date from the 1740s and is known to have been standing since c1780. The mill was working until it was struck by lightning in 1905 which damaged the sails and windshaft. In 1934 the derelict mill was restored by Neves the Heathfield millwrights as a memorial to the wife of Sir William Bird. Further repairs were done in 1954 by E. Hole and Sons, the Burgess Hill millwrights. It was restored again in 2004 and is now owned by West Sussex County Council.

The mill is a four-storey tower mill with a sixteen-sided beehive cap. Originally it was hand wound and later it had a fantail fitted, which was not replicated during restorations. The four common sails were originally carried on a wooden windshaft which was

Halnaker Windmill. The mill has a 16-sided beehive cap.

damaged by the 1905 lightning strike. A cast iron windshaft and wooden brake wheel from a wind sawmill at Punnets Town were fitted. The windshaft was cut in two pieces bolted together and was too short for Halnaker Mill; so, Neves inserted a spacer to strengthen it. The mill worked two pairs of overdrift (driven from above) millstones.

The mill has a 16-sided beehive cap.

The mill is a Grade II listed building and was further restored in 2018 with a new tile-hung façade and extensive repairs to the cap and balcony. The sails (or sweeps) have also been restored and rehung.

A few yards over from Halnaker Mill is an octagonal building that is often mistaken for a pillbox or gun emplacement. However, it is the remains of a High Frequency Direction Finding (HFDF) station from WWII as there were several RAF stations nearby at Goodwood, Tangmere and Merston.

Halnaker Mill and High Frequency Direction Finding station.

At the start of WWII, the only method of remotely determining the position of aircraft was using these towers. The brick enclosures would have protected a 3-storey wooden tower containing an aerial by which high frequency radio signals were exchanged with aircraft to guide them to their bases. The aerials could be rotated through 360 degrees by a 'steering wheel' housed in the cabin below.

Just to the south of the windmill, in the adjacent field, are the foundation remains of a WWII searchlight

Searchlight emplacement.

emplacement which adds to the strategic importance of Halnaker Hill.

For those of you that like to record and photograph trig points don't miss the one that is alongside the hedgerow.

Now you can do Walk 11a up to the windmill with some fantastic views. I will see you at Slindon to visit Nore Folly and 'crick'.

SUGGESTED WALK

WALK 11a. Halnaker Windmill (1.75 miles 2.8 km)

Parking. Small layby alongside the A285 by Warehead Farm. (Post code PO18 0NF.) This short walk is a there-and-back walk that is especially popular with children and at the weekends the parking area can get full up; so, try to do this walk on a weekday. Half the walk involves a steady climb up to reach the windmill and enjoy the views and the return journey is easy although there are four stiles. Walk 4 I said was the most beneficial walk so far as it helped you understand the layout of Chichester Harbour; this short walk is also very useful as from the top you have expansive views along the south coast and can see where you have walked so far and where the walks will continue.

As this is a short walk, I have considered Boxgrove and Halnaker as one walk as you can quite easily do them both on the same day with a very short drive between them. The total mileage for both is 4.25 miles (6.8km). There are no places for refreshments on this walk.

1. From the end of the layby, go along the wide gravel access road and climb gently between houses at first and then beneath a tunnel of trees. When you reach a metal gate, go over the stile that is to the right of it and continue ahead now climbing with a barbed wire fence on your right. Cross another stile and continue ahead. At a 3-way footpath sign go slightly left/ahead and in 20 yards you reach a swing gate by a footpath sign. Go through the gate and go left up the left edge of a field beside a hedgerow, that attracts butterflies, and soon you get the first glimpse of the top of Halnaker Windmill. Just keep climbing until you go through a gate and you have arrived.

This hedgerow is popular with butterflies.

2. From the windmill you are surrounded by extensive views across the south coast. Take your time here and as you look out you will see the English Channel, Isle of Wight, the top of the Spinnaker Tower at Portsmouth, Chichester Cathedral, the distinctive 'Millennium Dome' shapes of Butlin's in Bognor Regis and the Rampion Wind Farm; if you look carefully you can also work out Boxgrove Priory and ruins. On the far side of the windmill look out for the distinctive path between the trees which is known as Halnaker Gallop or Halnaker Ride. The sweeping grass track cuts through dense woodland and it was established by Lord George Bentinck in 1841 as a training ground for the Goodwood horses in preparation for racing competitions.

Trig point with NHS message of thanks.

Along the hedgerow you have the trig point which at the time of writing someone had chalked a message of thanks to the NHS for their efforts during the COVID-19 outbreak. Don't forget to have a look at the other stone building which is the High Frequency Direction Finding station and the foundation remains of the searchlight emplacement.

Halnaker Gallop (Ride).

3. Return the same way, walking down the field with the hedgerow on your right, through the swing gate, along the raised footpath to the left of the access road, then over a stile and follow the access road down to the start.

Boxgrove Priory and Guest House ruin.

SLINDON

Slindon is a rural village located about 6 miles northeast of Chichester. Much of Slindon's woodland belongs to the National Trust and it is on the southern edge of the escarpment of the South Downs National Park. Most of the village is managed by the Slindon Estate which is itself owned by the National Trust and as a result this means there is a higher than average emphasis on preventing development and keeping things as they are.

The village is listed in the Domesday Book as 'Eslindone' which it is thought is the Old English for 'sloping hill'. In the Middle Ages Slindon House, now Slindon College, was the site of one of the Archbishop of Canterbury's residences. In 1330 Thomas de Natindon, who was a legal representative of the Pope, was sent there to serve a writ on the archbishop. His party were not well received by the

archbishop's servants who stripped and bound them, then threw cold water over them, apparently with the archbishop's consent. Natindon escaped and was pursued over the hills to Petworth where he was caught and imprisoned for three days.

Nore Folly and trig point.

St Mary's twelfth century church has a memorial to Stephen Langton c1150–1228 who was the Archbishop of Canterbury who attended the signing of the Magna Carta.

In the mid-eighteenth century, Slindon Cricket Club achieved fame through the excellence of its team which featured Richard Newland (1718-91) who's memorial is in the church. No one knows where the first cricket match was played but it seems clear that it originated in the sheep-grazing counties of Southern England, where the short grass of the pastures made it possible to bowl a ball of wool or rags at a target; the target was usually the wicket-gate of the sheep pasture which was defended with a bat in the form of a shepherd's crooked staff. Slindon boasts perhaps the best claim to be the birthplace of cricket and its heritage is honoured by the memorial

St Mary's church.

of 'crick', a wicket, bat and ball. This is because Slindon Common with its clay surface on fast-draining gravel provided a fast and level pitch allowing more accurate play than the usual downland turf. The plaque on 'crick' reads:

'Crick' memorial.

THIS SIGN WAS DONATED BY
THE SLINDON PUDDING CLUB
AND DEPICTS THE SHAPE
AND SIZE
OF THE BAT AND WICKET
THAT WAS FIRST USED IN
SLINDON IN 1731

In May 2012, the process began of renovating and converting the old village forge into a shop, café and information centre that opened on sixteenth October 2012 and has become the focal point of the village after the local pub shut down. It is thought that the original building began as

The Forge.

a wheelwright's c1860 and was extended and converted into a full forge c1880.

Along with 'crick' Slindon is probably most famous for Nore Folly (Slindon Folly) which is a short walk from the village. It is a strange shaped structure that is difficult to describe. It's located on a small hill about half a mile from Slindon and one description of it says that it resembles an entrance to a non-existent tunnel and it is not known why it was built. However, during the second half of the eighteenth century Slindon was the family seat of the Countess of Newburgh and her husband, the third Earl. It has been suggested that it was built as a replica Italian arch, erected at the request of the Countess and based upon a painting that she owned. The National Trust, which restored the folly in 1993, states that Nore Folly was 'built in 1814 for the Countess of Newburgh's picnic parties'. At that time there was a small covered building attached, which has since been torn down. It is a Grade II listed building and the folly was featured on a first day cover designed by British First Day Covers Limited in 2006. The folly is reached on the associated walk via a fairly steep walking path and from the folly there are views of Halnaker Windmill, a long section of the West Sussex coastline, the Spinnaker Tower at Portsmouth, Chichester Cathedral and Butlin's at Bognor Regis. Again, for those of you that like to record and photograph trig points, don't miss the one that is in the open in front the folly.

Now you can do Walk 12 to see 'crick' and Nore Folly and I'll see you at Tortington for the 'beakhead' monsters.

SUGGESTED WALK

WALK 12. Nore Folly and 'crick' (5.0 miles 8.0 km)

Parking. There is roadside parking just up from (not outside or too close too) The Forge village shop/café. (Post code BN18 0QT.) This walk is fairly hilly with a couple of short but steep climbs but there are no stiles. The walk starts by passing the 'crick' then enters Nore Woods on the way to Nore Folly. From here there are lovely views including areas you have already walked; if you look at the sea in front you, you will see Butlin's at Bognor. Refreshments are available from The Forge.

1. With your back to The Forge shop/café go left and walk up the road using the left-hand pavement and, in a few yards, you reach 'crick' on a small green on the left-hand side. There is a plaque on 'crick' which is worth reading.

Plaque on 'crick' memorial.

Cross Park Lane and continue ahead up School Hill. Go past Church Hill on the left (this is where you finish the walk) and at the top follow the road around to the left. In a few yards turn right up Mill Lane and when it bends to the right, go ahead through a double gateway up a track as signposted by a Public Bridleway sign. As you go keep a look out on the left for a distant view of Nore Folly. Enter tree cover and continue downhill staying on the path below the tree cover. At a 3-way footpath sign, (not the 4-way sign to the right signposted as 'Bridle Road to Bignor') continue ahead downhill soon reaching another 3-way signpost. Continue ahead with a wire fence and open field on your right.

2. At a 3-way signpost with an iron gate a few yards further ahead, turn left and descend quite steeply. The path soon opens up and Nore Folly is in view on the hill ahead. Follow the

Nore Folly from a distance.

path downhill and when it enters the tree cover of Nore Wood continue ahead.

Airfield memorial.

Soon you reach a lane where you turn right. When the lane bends right by a small parking area, continue ahead (slightly left) along the bridleway as directed by a 2-way signpost. Just follow the track, passing a plaque saying 'In Memory of Slindon Airfield' and go left at a 4-way signpost that is beneath an oak tree. Follow the bridleway down into the woodland, and then start to climb quite steeply. Ignore a 3-way footpath sign on your right, continue climbing and at a junction go left as directed by a blue arrow on a marker post on your right.

Climb up the wide track and at the top of the climb, at a junction, go left. In 25 yards, at a marker post, go left around a wooden barrier and continue beneath tall tree cover. Stay on this path and follow it out of Nore Wood via a wide metal gate that will probably be open. Follow the path around to the right and appreciate the far-reaching views as you curve around. If you look carefully you can clearly see the white conical tent-like roofs of Butlin's Holiday Park on the coast at Bognor Regis. Then, without warning, Nore Folly is just there a few yards away on your right, standing prominently over all she surveys. Easily overlooked, although it is in the open, there is a trig point so make sure you get that in your photo as well. There is also a conveniently located bench for you to sit and admire the views.

3. To start the return journey, follow the wide stony access track downhill, remembering to have regular look-backs for a different perspective and appreciation of Nore Folly and Halnaker Windmill can be seen to your right. At a junction of tracks, go left and just follow it to reach a lane. Taking care, turn right up the quiet lane and follow it around to the left to reach a road. Go left and follow the road around to the right, passing Slindon College on the right and St Richard's Catholic church on the left.

At a road junction, go right down Church Hill passing St Mary's church and then a pond on the right. Just follow the quiet road to reach a road at the end. Turn right down the road which was used on the outward journey, re-pass 'crick' back to the start.

St Richard's Catholic church.

TORTINGTON

Tortington is a small village that lies between Arundel and Ford by the River Arun. Arundel Castle is a dominant landmark that is clearly visible from Tortington and the River Arun flows for a few miles south where it joins the English Channel at Littlehampton.

Tortington is an ancient manor and parish beside the River Arun. The parish was originally shaped like an inverted triangle but many boundary changes took place over the centuries. As well as the manor there was a medieval Augustinian monastery – Tortington Priory. A church was first mentioned in the mid-twelfth century when there was a rectory and it was built primarily to serve the priory.

The doorway and chancel arch at St Mary Magdalene's church are from that era and both date to c1140, the layout and fabric of the church are still largely twelfth century despite subsequent restoration. An aisle with two bays was added to the south side of the nave in the thirteenth century and the door was moved to accommodate it. During or before the eighteenth century the aisle was destroyed and its arcade was blocked. Another thirteenth century change was the addition of lancet windows in the north and south walls of the chancel.

In the fifteenth and sixteenth centuries seating was installed for parishioners and some of these seats survive in the form of plain, straight-headed wooden benches. Features that were described in the medieval period but which are now lost include a Lady chapel (but a recess on the outside of the chancel wall may be a remnant of this), a leaded steeple and a porch of which there are fragmentary remains. A white bell-turret replaced the steeple; constructed of timber and added in the eighteenth century, it was reputedly painted white to help with navigation along the River Arun. Also, in the eighteenth century the chancel arch and chancel roof were remodelled.

The main reason I have highlighted this church is for the 'beakhead' monsters. The highlight of this lovely little church is its ancient chancel arch which is of the same date as the font but of a completely different design; the influence here

St Mary Magdalene's church.

Chancel arch with 'Beakhead' monster carvings.

coming from Scandinavian or pagan tradition. This type of carving is known as 'beakhead' and it is easy to see why. There are two bands of masonry – the outer band being formed of bird's beaks which grip a roll moulding. The leaves or feathers from which the heads grow have a variety of designs, some bird-like, one a rabbit, many topped with feathers, foliage or tentacles. These creatures would have originally been brightly painted to inspire awe and wonder, perhaps fear, in the congregation praying below. The church was listed as Grade II by English Heritage on 5 June 1958.

'Beakhead' monsters around Chancel arch.

The River Arun is 37 miles (60km) long and is the longest river that is entirely within Sussex. From a series of streams that form its source in the area of St Leonard's Forest in the Weald, the Arun flows westwards through Horsham to Nowhurst where it is joined by the North River. Turning south it is joined by its main tributary, the western River Rother, and continues through a gap in the South Downs to Arundel to join the English Channel at Littlehampton. The Arun is one of the fastest flowing rivers in England and is tidal as far inland as Pallingham Quay which is 25.5 miles (41 km) upstream from the sea at Littlehampton. The Arun gives its name to the Arun local government district of West Sussex.

The mouth of the river has not always been at Littlehampton. Up until the late fifteenth century it joined the River Adur at Lancing some 10 miles to the east before entering the sea. This estuary became blocked with shingle by the eastward drift of the tides, pushing the Adur towards Shoreham-by-Sea, while the Arun broke out at Worthing, Goring and Ferring at various times, until it formed its present-day estuary at Littlehampton between 1500 and 1530. Littlehampton and its harbour were guarded from attack by Littlehampton Redoubt on the western bank at the mouth of the river. It was completed in 1854 and is now screened from the sea by Climping sand dunes. This fort replaced a seven-gun battery on the east bank which was built in 1764. (Described and walked past in Chapter 11 – Climping.)

Arundel Castle and River Arun.

Now it's time for you to do Walk 13 where you will see the 'beakhead' monsters and walk alongside the River Arun enjoying the view of Arundel Castle and looking out for the wildlife. I will see you a short distance away along the river at Arundel.

SUGGESTED WALK

WALK 13. 'Beakhead' Monsters and River Arun (4.25 miles 6.80 km)

Parking. There is roadside parking along Priory Road by the ends of Wood View or Howard Road. (Postcode BN18 9EJ.) This walk is mainly level as it is beside the River Arun but there is a hilly section at the very start where there are also two stiles to cross. The walk takes you to the 'Beakhead' monsters at St Mary Magdalene's church before heading across to the banks of the River Arun for the return journey. Refreshments are not available on this walk.

1. Walk down Priory Road until you turn left up Wood View. Follow the road to its end and go left up Kirdford Road, not signed. Go up to the end of the road and go left along Torton Hill, not signed. In 35 yards, go right along Pearson Road and in 20 yards go left at a footpath sign. Go to the left of a row of five garages and over a stile beside a wide metal gate. Go ahead up the left edge of a field and cross a stile on the far side. Go through trees and in a few yards, you reach a 3-way footpath sign, continue ahead with houses to your left. Cross a minor junction and continue ahead on a slightly more curving path but always along the path with the houses close on your left. When you reach the end, go ahead on an enclosed path between fence panels to reach a road. Turn right along the road and in about 40 yards, go left along Birch Close. At the end of Birch Close, go through a small metal gate to reach a minor lane.

2. Go left down the quiet lane and follow it as it gradually curves to the left. At a footpath sign on the right by Hanger Down House/Brooklands, go right along the private drive and when you reach the entrance to Priory Manor, step to the right and continue ahead to the right of the wooden fence.

Cross a bridge by a 3-way footpath sign and go straight ahead across the left edge of a large field; if there are crops growing mind your footing as the crops sometimes come right up to the field edge. As you cross the field there is a good view of the rear of Tortington Manor on your left. On the far side of the field you

Tortington Manor.

reach Tortington Lane, not signed. Go left along the lane and just follow it passing Tortington Manor on the left. Just a few yards past the end of the grounds to Tortington Manor you reach a footpath sign on the left. Go left here passing a pond on the right then continuing directly ahead across the grass (with a lovely view of the manor on the left) and go along a short track into the trees opposite to reach a 2-way footpath sign. (Please do not deviate from this path as the area is strictly private.) Turn right and go directly ahead towards the church in sight. Go through the gate into St Mary Magdalene's church and visit it if only to see the carvings of the 'Beakhead' monsters – try to imagine them brightly painted.

3. Leave the church by the main gate, go ahead a few paces, then go right between hedgerows back to Tortington Lane. Turn left down the lane to reach Ford Road at the end. Cross the road and go directly ahead along a wide access track across a field to the raised riverbank in view. On the far side go up the grass bank to reach the bank of the River Arun. Now go left and just follow the path beside the meandering river, enjoying the views of Arundel Castle and Cathedral as you go. As you walk along the riverbank keep a look out for the

'Beakhead' monsters, originally brightly painted.

varied birdlife and butterflies which can be numerous during the summer months. Swans and black-headed gulls are very common here.

Just stay on the riverbank path and eventually, when you are about 100 yards short of South Marsh Mill, on the other side of the river, go left at a 3-way footpath sign and ahead between trees to reach Ford Road. Turn right along the road using the left-hand pavement and go left up Maxwell Road. At a mini roundabout go right along Priory Road and at the next mini roundabout keep right back to the start.

Arundel Castle and Cathedral.

Oystercatcher.

103

ARUNDEL

Arundel is a picture postcard market town in a steep vale of the South Downs dominated by the prominent and imposing Arundel Castle. Situated a short distance from Tortington the hilly town is packed with Georgian and Victorian houses and the high street is full of unusual independent shops. The River Arun runs through the eastern side of the town and a short distance north of the castle the Arundel Wildfowl and Wetlands Centre is an important birdlife conservation centre. The town is well known for its castle and Roman Catholic Cathedral that both dominate the local skyline and although smaller, Arundel has a museum and comes second behind much larger Chichester for its number of listed buildings.

The name Arundel comes from the Old English Harhunedell, 'valley of horehound' and is recorded in the Domesday Book. However, popular etymology connects the name with the Old French word arondelle 'swallow', a diminutive form of arunde or aronde, and swallows appear on the town's arms.

Arundel Castle.

The town is a major bridging point over the River Arun as it was the lowest road bridge until the opening of the Littlehampton swing bridge in 1908. The town itself lies outside of the boundaries of the South Downs National Park. On the 6 July 2004, Arundel was granted Fairtrade Town status. The town is home to one of the oldest Scout Groups in the world. 1st Arundel (Earl of Arundel's Own) Scout Group was formed in 1908 only a few weeks after Scouting began. It also has its own cricket ground at the castle, often referred to as one of the country's most picturesque; it hosts Sussex County Cricket Club for a number of games each season. People born in Arundel are known locally as Mullets, due to the large number of mullets in the River Arun and the local football team are nicknamed The Mullets.

Arundel Castle is a restored medieval castle founded by Roger de Montgomery on Christmas Day 1067. He became the first to hold the earldom of Arundel by the graces of William the Conqueror. The castle was damaged in the English Civil War and then restored in the eighteenth and nineteenth centuries. Since the eleventh century the castle has served as a hereditary stately home and has been in the family of the Duke of Norfolk for over 400 years. It is still the principle seat of the Norfolk family. Work began on the castle in 1067 during the reign of William the Conqueror as a fortification for the mouth of the River Arun at Littlehampton (about 4 miles away) and as a defensive position for the surrounding land against invasion from France. The original structure was a motte and double bailey castle.

The castle is set in 40 acres of sweeping grounds and gardens and has been open to visitors seasonally for nearly 200 years. It is home to priceless works of art, furniture, tapestries, stained glass, china, clocks, sculpture, carvings, heraldry and armour all in stunning room settings. Telephone +44 (0) 1903 882173 for opening times and prices.

The Priory Church of St Nicholas is deceptively large and unique. Deceptive because from the outside the church looks big but inside it is split at the crossing with one half screened off and access is only via the castle. It is unique because the parish half is Anglican and the castle half (the Fitzalan Chapel) is Roman Catholic; the separation is by an iron grille.

St Nicholas church.

The Cathedral Church of Our Lady and St Philip Howard is a Roman Catholic Cathedral. It was dedicated in 1873 as the Catholic parish church of Arundel and it became a cathedral at the foundation of the Diocese of Arundel and Brighton in 1965. It now serves as the seat of the Bishop of Arundel and Brighton.

Cathedral church of Our Lady and St Philip Howard.

Hiorne Tower.

Hiorne Tower is a folly located in Arundel Park very close to Arundel Castle. The three-sided castellated structure was built in 1787 by Francis Hiorne and from here there are lovely views across the South Downs. Hiorne built the tower to demonstrate his architectural ability to the Duke of Norfolk so that he could take charge of the renovation of Arundel Castle. There is not much information about his life or any other buildings he may have worked on and he died before he could do any more work for the duke. The tower is reputed to be haunted and

was used in the filming of Doctor Who featuring the Cybermen in June 1988.

The Blackfriars or Dominican priory was founded in the second quarter of the thirteenth century, perhaps by Isabel, Countess of Arundel. Friars liked to live close to the people they were preaching to and here they were beside not only the river crossing but also the port and market. Many other priories had low-lying sites on the edge of a town or city, for instance the London Blackfriars. The function of the surviving south range is not clear but since it was two-storeyed it

Blackfriars priory ruins.

cannot have contained the church; that must have been in the north range, remains of which can be seen above. The west range which has mostly gone may have included the dormitory; nothing is known about the east range if there was one. After the priory was dissolved in 1538 its buildings were converted to other uses: the south range for a while contained a timber yard and the west range a malthouse. Mill Road was laid out across the site in 1894. The remains of the south range were given to the town by the 16th Duke of Norfolk in 1935.

Swanbourne Lake.

Swanbourne Lodge Tea Room.

Swanbourne Lodge is located at the gateway of the 1000-acre Arundel Park overlooking the boating lake with a backdrop of cliffs and trees. The lodge was built in 1852 and is one of the best examples of a split flintstone building in Sussex. Today it is a tea room that serves cream teas and homemade cakes. This area is a haven for plants and wildlife such as local and exotic water birds, water rats, voles, bats and dragonflies.

Now you can do Walk 14 where you can explore all of Arundel including Hiorne Tower, Swanbourne Lake and the River Arun. I will see you back at the West Sussex coast at Middleton-on-Sea to continue the coastal journey along to reach the River Arun where it meets the sea at Littlehampton Harbour by the Climping sand dunes.

SUGGESTED WALK

WALK 14. Arundel Castle, Cathedral, Hiorne Tower, Swanbourne Lake & River Arun (4.75 miles 7.6 km).

Parking. There is free roadside parking along Mill Road on the right-hand side if you arrive early or the pay-and-display car park in Mill Road. (Post code BN18 9PA.) This is a fairly easy walk with loads to see. The first part of the walk involves a steady climb up the High Street to reach the cathedral and Hiorne Tower but then it is all downhill or level with only one stile. Refreshments are available in Arundel or Swanbourne Tea Room overlooking the lake.

1. Cross over Mill Road and go left walking beside the little stream on your right with lovely views of Arundel Castle up above. Look out for ducks here especially the mandarin duck.

Soon you reach the castle entrance and just past the entrance on the left are the ruins of Blackfriars Priory. At a mini roundabout go right and walk up the High Street passing shops, bars, cafés etc. Go up the hill and at the top you have the castle walls on your right.

Arundel Castle.

Follow the road around to the left and just past the main castle wall you reach the fourteenth century Priory Church of St Nicholas on the right. Continue along the road for a few more yards to reach the Cathedral Church of Our Lady and St Philip Howard which is another prominent landmark for the surrounding area. Next to the Cathedral is the St Mary's Gate Inn which is ideally situated for refreshments before your walk through Arundel Park.

Mandarin duck in the stream below Arundel Castle.

2. Continue along the road and soon after passing St Philip's School on the left, go right up the access road into Arundel Park. Please keep to the designated paths and keep dogs on a lead as the surrounding land is privately owned and has grazing animals. Follow the access road, climbing gently, and pass through a gate between stone pillars which is beside a stone gatehouse. Continue ahead up the main access road and soon after it bends left, go right at the Footpath sign across the grass to reach the three-sided Hiorne Tower, passing a stone memorial on the way.

Hiorne Tower and memorial.

Swanbourne Lake.

3. Continue past the tower to reach a pathway with a low fence on the other side and lovely views beyond. Go right along the path and immediately after the fence ends go left down beneath trees; there is also a footpath sign at the end of the fence to direct you. In a few yards go left over a stile, which is to the right of a gate, and go ahead along the wide chalk path with a limited view of the tail-end of Swanbourne Lake in the valley below. Follow the path as it gradually descends; on your right at the bottom of the valley you can see the path which you will soon be walking along.

At the end of the descent you reach a junction of paths where you turn sharp right to follow the previously mentioned path at the bottom of the valley. Just stay on this path and soon you pass through a swing gate at the start of Swanbourne Lake; soon after passing through the swing gate you get a final glimpse of the top of Hiorne Tower on the hill behind the lake. Continue ahead, staying on this path, with the lake on your right and eventually you reach the lovely Swanbourne Lodge Tea Room next to the entrance and when open there is also the chance to hire a boat.

4. Go through the entrance/exit gate and turn right along the road. At the very start of the hump-backed bridge, go left down steps by a footpath sign. (If you do not want to do this part of the walk you can continue along the road back to the start.) Do not cross the footbridge but go ahead along the path with the river on your right and at the end of the path you reach the banks of the River Arun. Turn right and follow the river with lovely views of Arundel Castle on the right. Just follow the river bank clockwise in a wide sweeping

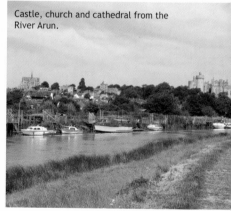

Castle, church and cathedral from the River Arun.

circle ignoring a footpath off to the right. Eventually, as if by magic, the castle, church and cathedral all appear directly in front of you making for a good photograph.

Go through a swing gate and continue beside the river. Go right through the car park out to Mill Road at the start almost opposite the castle entrance which is just a few yards to your left.

CHAPTER 11
MIDDLETON-ON-SEA, ELMER & CLIMPING SAND DUNES

Old wreck at Littlehampton Harbour from Climping.

Beach at Middleton-on-Sea.

MIDDLETON-ON-SEA

Middleton-on Sea is a village to the east of Bognor Regis and Felpham. Although the beach is one of the sunniest spots in the United Kingdom its coastline is relatively quiet and peaceful; the reason being is that there are only a few access points and virtually no facilities. At low tide there are large expanses of sand and the beach includes substantial sea defences against coastal erosion including wooden groynes and a sea wall. Restaurants and shops can be found in Middleton-on-Sea itself including three local pubs one of which the Beresford is named after Viscount William Beresford who was a general in the British army and also a commander of the Portuguese armed forces; the image of William Beresford is on the pub's sign.

The ancient parish which was just called Middleton had 370 acres in 1881 but had been reduced in area from previous centuries by sea erosion. The configuration of the western and northern boundaries suggest that the parish was once part of Felpham and the name Middleton may refer to the manor's central position between Felpham and either Elmer or Cudlow in Climping. Part of the eastern boundary was formed c1310 by a ditch and part by Elmer pool, while the north-eastern boundary follows the Ryebank Rife. The parish was extended in 1933 by the addition of Ancton from Felpham parish and in 1971 it had 892 acres; it was in 1934 that its name was extended to Middleton-on-Sea to prevent confusion with any other Middletons.

In 1910 engineer Norman Thompson, who was attracted to the area by the large expanse of firm sand and the constant winds along the shore, founded an aircraft works which after the removal of much of the sand in a storm in 1913 turned to making

Middleton-on-Sea towards Elmer.

seaplanes; the firm was later called Norman Thompson Flight Co. During WWI it supplied aircraft to the Navy, the workforce growing from ten to between 700 and 900. About 250 aircraft were built but with the cancellation of orders at the end of WWI the firm went into liquidation.

In the 1920s Middleton became a popular holiday destination. The 'New City' created by Sir Walter Blount, opened in 1922 in the former seaplane factory south of the church and it was one of the earliest attempts to provide a self-contained environment for enjoying the seaside. It consisted of around 200 bedrooms all with central heating and half with private baths beside a garage for 100 cars; visitors without cars could be met at Barnham Station. Almost every form of amusement was catered for; one of the hangars accommodated a dance hall and another had indoor tennis courts. There were also outdoor tennis courts, a putting green, and rooms for cards and billiards. The New City had its own dairy, farm, ice generating plant and mineral water factory as well as a laundry, hairdressing rooms and a lending library. By the mid-1920s it was said to be very popular with large numbers of distinguished visitors.

St Nicholas church, Middleton-on-Sea.

There was a church at Middleton in 1086. By the late eighteenth century most of the chancel had been destroyed by the sea, the south aisle demolished and its arcade filled in, and part of the west end including the tower removed. Repairs were carried out in 1803 but in 1804 there were rarely more than six or seven in the congregation. A very high tide early in 1838 virtually destroyed what was left of the building making it unusable, the ruins survived in 1847 but had disappeared by 1849. The new church with the same dedication to St Nicholas was consecrated in 1849 and is built on a site given by Richard Coote, Lord of Middleton Manor, safely away from the sea.

ELMER

Elmer is a coastal village and a very close neighbour of Middleton-on-Sea. Elmer Sands beach is a steep bank of pebbles expanding into flat compacted sand when the tide is out. There are a number of rock sea defences which become interesting rock pools and islands at low tide making them ideal to explore for shells, shrimps and crabs. The beach is hard to get access to due to the private beach-side estates that are common on this part of the coast. There are no facilities but there are

Elmer beach towards Climping.

shops and pubs located on the main road which is just back from the beach.

The whole area of Elmer used to be farmland until the housing drive of the post-war years when the Elmer Sands Estate was built. Much of the original housing in the Elmer Sands Estate consisted of old railway carriages but over the years these have been replaced with modern housing.

During the early nineteenth century Damien Cox, a British Archaeologist, discovered the fossilised remains of *sus domesticus* (domestic pig) whilst excavating in the beach area; the fossils are now held in the local Post Office.

CLIMPING SAND DUNES (WEST BEACH DUNES)

Climping also spelt Clymping is a village containing agricultural and natural sandy land and the parish also contains the coastal hamlet of Atherington. Fringing the coast towards the River Arun at Littlehampton are the Climping sand dunes (West Beach dunes) a Site of Special Scientific Interest, which includes areas of rare vegetated shingle.

Climping beach from sand dunes towards Elmer.

Climping beach from sand dunes towards Littlehampton Harbour.

Climbing beach is also referred to as Atherington beach after the coastal hamlet it sits within rather than the nearby village of Climping. The beach has pebbles at high tide, is divided by wooden groynes but at low tide there is a huge expanse of dark, fine, hard-packed sand. Climping beach is quieter than its neighbouring beach at Littlehampton and as you walk along the beach towards Littlehampton (as you will on the associated walk) much of the area is designated as scientific interest and parts are a nature reserve with areas of the sand dunes fenced off to protect them against erosion and to help local species to thrive. The actual beach is exposed and struggles with coastal erosion to such an extent that its appearance can change between visits. There is a large pay-for parking area (where you will start the associated walk) at the end of Climping Street which has a café and toilets and it is that section of the beach which is most badly affected by erosion.

Climping sand dunes.

Golf course on the other side of the dunes.

Vegetation on the Climping sand dunes include marram grass which is essential for the dunes to work and dominate the stabilised parts of the dunes; other grasses include dune fescue and red fescue. The dunes support important populations of wintering birds and the numbers of wintering sanderling, in particular, are of European significance; vegetated shingle beaches are a nationally uncommon habitat. Plant communities include yellow horned poppy, sea kale, sea beet, curled dock, eryngium maritimum, sand catchfly, viper's bugloss and Nottingham catchfly.

Littlehampton Fort is located at the end of Rope Walk behind Climping sand dunes by the golf course. A path runs up through the sand dunes where you can see the southernmost part of the fort or you can view it with binoculars or a zoom camera from Littlehampton across the harbour as I did. The fort is over 165 years old and is currently listed as a Scheduled Monument and Building at Risk with Historic England. The sand dunes to the south of the fort have given it protection from the southerly winds which means the fort is still in good condition. It is however under threat as it is overwhelmed by vegetation which is causing damage to the remaining structures and putting the future of the fort at risk.

The fort belongs to a class of military installation termed 'batteries' – self-contained positions where guns were mounted for purposes of offensive or defensive action: the object being primarily to bring guns to bear on a specific area, to provide the appropriate range and to protect the guns (and crew) during action. Ammunition would usually be stored behind the rampart (the area known as the 'gorge') and by the later nineteenth century in purpose-built magazines. The fort is built of red brick and pebble and includes a lunette battery for three 68 pounder guns and two 32 pounder guns, which is surrounded by a detached Carnot wall with three open bastions defended by musket loops. Although largely covered by sand the Carnot wall is thought to survive to full height with original coping. The exterior moat is filled with sand but survives as a buried feature. The barrack block and offices to the rear were partially demolished c1965 but the foundations are still visible. Littlehampton Fort is similar in design to Shoreham Fort but the Carnot wall has open bastions instead of caponiers.

Littlehampton Fort was built to replace a gun battery which had been constructed in 1764 on the east side of the harbour; this was dismantled c1834 and became a coastguard station. The new fort was built by a London firm, Messrs Lock and Wesham under the supervision of Captain Fenwick of the Royal Engineers between February and September 1854. It was planned to accommodate two infantry officers, one master gunner, forty-two Non-Commissioned Officers and a further thirty Non-Commissioned Officers in a small building outside the fort on the north side. The five guns were probably installed after the Crimean War (1853-1865) but the fort was taken out of action in 1873. The fort was almost certainly re-fortified during WWII and an observation post was built nearby between 1940 and 1941.

Now you can do Walk 15 to see Climping sand dunes and Littlehampton Harbour before I see you on the other side of the harbour to explore Littlehampton.

Littlehampton Fort as seen from across the harbour.

SUGGESTED WALK

WALK 15. Climping Sand Dunes and Littlehampton Harbour
(4.25 miles 6.8 km)

Parking. Pay-for car park at the end of Climping Street. The walk can be done in less than two hours). This is a fairly easy walk only made slightly more difficult by having to walk on pebbles between the parking area and Littlehampton Harbour. There are no stiles. Refreshments are available from the café at the parking area or at the café by Littlehampton Harbour.

1. From the end of the car park go left along a raised shingle bank to reach a 3-way footpath sign in about 75 yards. (As you can see this area is constantly battered by the elements and it can look different between visits). Continue ahead along the top of the beach just aiming for Littlehampton Harbour which is clearly visible ahead. At the next signpost continue ahead but there is an information board to the left on a stone base giving you information about the area (this is also the point that you will come back to on your return journey).

Continue with a wire fence on your left and a brief view of what remains of

Climping's eroding beach by car park.

View across the harbour to Littlehampton.

Climping Windmill which is now a private residence. (The wire fences that surround some of the sand dunes are because they are protected areas but there are still plenty of dunes which you can climb and, in case you are wondering, behind the dunes is Littlehampton Golf Course.) Just before the harbour wall there is an alternate path that goes up between the dunes to arrive by Littlehampton Fort but the walk continues right up to the harbour with good views across it to Littlehampton which gets packed on hot, sunny days.

2. From the harbour go left to a car park, you can continue beside the harbour with the lighthouse on your right and good views of the boats ahead. When you

reach a sign in front of you saying 'Private', go left to reach the entrance to the car park. Go right up Rope Walk using the right-hand path on the narrow stretch of grass and pass Littlehampton Yacht Club on your right. Stay on the path which rises beside the road and just follow it beside the harbour with lovely views including an area with minor shipwrecks. Just follow this path until it ends back at Rope Walk.

Littlehampton Harbour.

3. Immediately cross the road and go along the footpath that is directly opposite. The path continues ahead through trees with Littlehampton Golf Course on your left, you are warned about stray balls. Just follow this path and eventually you reach a 3-way footpath sign. Continue ahead beside the golf course to arrive back at the beach beside the information board you passed on the outward journey. Turn right along the top of the beach and follow it back to the car park.

Retractable bridge across harbour.

Shipwreck beside the footpath.

CHAPTER 12
LITTLEHAMPTON, RUSTINGTON, FERRING & GORING-BY-SEA

Littlehampton retractable footbridge.

LITTLEHAMPTON

Littlehampton is a seaside town and pleasure harbour that sits on the eastern bank of the mouth of the River Arun. A human settlement can be traced back to prehistoric and Roman times and it appears in the Domesday Book of 1086 as the small hamlet of Hantone. It is believed to have been a fishing community around this time and appeared on a French map in c1100 as Hanton. It was then thought to have been given to the Abbey of St Martin de Seez in Normandy who owned Littlehampton until c1400. The area was then passed back to the ownership of successive Earls of Arundel and Dukes of Norfolk, whose successors still reside in Arundel today.

Littlehampton began to develop as a port as a result of the constant silting of the River Arun (the River Arun is described in Chapter 10 – Tortington) perhaps leading to the prefix of 'Little' being added to 'Hampton' in order to distinguish it from the larger Southampton further along the coast. The port expansion led to a new river mouth being cut in 1735 alongside the building of a wooden harbour; at this time, it was also known as Arundel Port.

Littlehampton looking towards Rustington.

Looking towards the harbour and Climping.

During the eighteenth century the town developed from a fishing community to a holiday destination and the town's status as both a port and a holiday resort led to economic success in the nineteenth century with a new railway line and a cross-channel ferry to Honfleur (near Le Havre) in France being introduced. Littlehampton remained as a holiday resort in the twentieth century and became known as 'The Children's Paradise' in the 1920s.

After the war Littlehampton saw large-scale house building on the outskirts of the town and eventually absorbed the surrounding villages of Wick, Lyminster and Toddington and the commercial element of the town became focused on boat building and water sports. Littlehampton has a mile-long sand and shingle beach with a promenade, well maintained seafront gardens and, at 1000ft, the UK's longest bench that runs along the seafront. The Long Bench is made from wood

and stainless steel and flows along the promenade curving around lamp posts and obstacles, twisting up into the shelters and dropping down to paths and crossings. It was opened in July 2010 and can seat over 300 people. Located right on the beachfront with views across the beach and the English Channel is the unusual and unique East Beach Café. Thomas Heatherwick rose to prominence early in his career when he was discovered by Sir Terence Conran straight out of the Royal College of Art. Conran lent his workshops to the upcoming designer to develop

Part of the 1000ft winding bench.

his early projects; Conran once called him 'the Leonardo da Vinci of our times'. Thomas set up Heatherwick Studio in 1994 bringing together architects, product designers and engineers within a single practice. The studio produced many successful product and installation designs but it was not until it was commissioned in September 2005 to create a new café on the beach at Littlehampton that it was able to complete a real building. Thomas and his design team, headed by Peter Ayres, created a structure that not only became a popular local café but was published around the world, attracting thousands of tourists to Littlehampton.

East Beach café.

Littlehampton port is based around the River Arun which flows into the English Channel. There has been a port here since Roman times and its history reflects physical, economic and social change over the centuries. It is a small but busy port that caters for active yachting, sport fishing, commercial fishing and larger commercial traffic. It is an ideal destination for cruising and can act as a gateway to historic Arundel and the South Downs National Park. Beside the harbour entrance is a short pier and a lighthouse which offer good views of the boats as they cruise in and out of the harbour.

Short pier beside harbour.

Further up the harbour is the Littlehampton Retractable Footbridge. The new footbridge was built in 1981 at a cost of half a million pounds and features a 120-ton retracting centrepiece that withdraws past the control tower. This allows large ships to dock in the port and it is opened on average 500 times a year by request to the Harbour Office.

Harbour entrance.

Right: Lighthouse on pier.

RUSTINGTON

Rustington is a town to the east of Littlehampton and the parish includes the neighbourhood of West Preston. Typically, its beaches consist of shingle divided up by a series of wooden groynes. As the tide goes out it reveals an expanse of flat sand which makes it popular with families but not as crowded as neighbouring Littlehampton.

During WWI Rustington was home to an American air base to the east of the High Street. It was intended to launch bombing raids against Germany but the airfield was incomplete when the war ended.

Typical flint and thatched house in The Street.

Rustington contains a conservation area which extends from the south end of North Lane to The Lamb pub in The Street. Along here trees are protected and there are the largest number of pre-1850 listed buildings in the town, with The Street and surrounding roads containing some of the finest seventeenth and eighteenth century Sussex flint cottages in West Sussex, some of which are thatched.

Rustington has been occupied since the Stone Age, through the Bronze Age, Iron Age, Roman and Medieval periods up to today. It is mentioned in the Domesday Book when it was part of land given to Roger de Montgomery following the Norman Conquest and he became Lord of the Manor. It remained as a small agricultural community throughout this time under successive Lords but things started to change with the mechanisation of farming and the railway station at Angmering opening in 1846. With the death of the last Lord of the Manor in 1868 the land was divided up and sold.

Many famous people have made their home or spent time in Rustington including Sir Hubert Parry of 'Jerusalem' fame who had his house Knightscroft

Plaques to Sir Hubert Parry and his wife by Knightscroft.

built in the village and lived there for forty years. The author and playwright J. M. Barrie, the creator of Peter Pan, stayed annually with the Du Maurier and Davies families at Cudlow House. There are blue plaques to remind us of those properties and both are down Sea Lane on opposite sides of the road.

Two air speed records were set over the seafront at Rustington. The first was achieved in September 1946 when Group Captain Teddy Donaldson flying a Gloster Meteor Star reached 615.78 mph (991 km/h) – he also became the first man to exceed 1000Km/h. The second was in September 1953 when Squadron Leader Neville Duke flying a Hawker Hunter WB188 set a speed of 727.63 mph (1170.9 km/h). To celebrate, on 7 September 1996, Neville Duke returned to Rustington to unveil a plaque to mark the event, joined by a Gloster Meteor and a Hawker Hunter which flew over the seafront.

Plaque to J. M. Barrie at Cudlow House.

FERRING

Ferring is a village to the east of Rustington and to the west of Goring-by-Sea. Ferring beach is located just beyond the Goring end of the long Worthing seafront and again consists of pebbles with sand at low tide divided up with wooden groynes. The beach is ideal for swimming at high tide and rock-pooling at low tide. The beach often has horse riders in the early morning as they gain access from the nearby Goring Gap Beach.

Ferring beach towards Goring-by-Sea.

A slightly more unexpected addition to Ferring beach is the Type 26 Pillbox which can be found at the top of the beach. Built in 1941 as part of a network of defences built all over the British Isles to prevent an anticipated invasion during WWII it is one of a few remaining examples and is identified as a structure of character and historical importance – there is a plaque on it to this effect.

The site of the village is an ancient one and the name itself is Saxon; the '-ing' termination being widespread over Sussex (the land of the South Saxons), denoting 'people of'. This was the settlement of a leader called Ferra. The village is mentioned in the Domesday Book and the parish church is Norman and dedicated to St Andrew. In the churchyard are buried the ashes of Major John Bigelow Dodge (1894–1960) who was a veteran of the Great Escape of 1944.

Until the 1920s the village was small but when the south coast began to be built-up, particularly with holiday homes, Ferring began to increase in size.

Type 26 Pillbox at the top of Ferring beach.

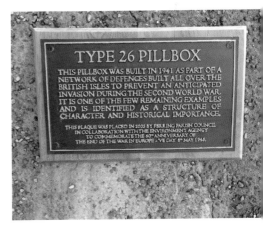

TYPE 26 PILLBOX

THIS PILLBOX WAS BUILT IN 1941 AS PART OF A NETWORK OF DEFENCES BUILT ALL OVER THE BRITISH ISLES TO PREVENT AN ANTICIPATED INVASION DURING THE SECOND WORLD WAR. IT IS ONE OF THE FEW REMAINING EXAMPLES AND IS IDENTIFIED AS A STRUCTURE OF CHARACTER AND HISTORICAL IMPORTANCE.

THIS PLAQUE WAS PLACED IN 2005 BY FERRING PARISH COUNCIL IN COLLABORATION WITH THE ENVIRONMENT AGENCY TO COMMEMORATE THE 60TH ANNIVERSARY OF THE END OF THE WAR IN EUROPE - 'VE DAY' 8TH MAY 1945.

GORING-BY-SEA

Goring-by-Sea, usually just referred to as Goring lies to the east of Ferring and to the west of Worthing. Historically in Sussex, in the Rape of Arundel, Goring has been part of Worthing since 1929. It is thought that the place-name Goring may mean either 'Gāra's people', or 'people of the wedge-shaped strip of land'. Usually known as Goring, the by-Sea suffix has been added to differentiate it from the village of Goring-on-Thames in Oxfordshire. The beach is a classic West Sussex beach with a long stretch of pebbles separated by wooden groynes with exposed flat sand when the tide is out. Behind the beach is a large grassy area which is separated from the beach by a narrow-paved strip that runs from the Sea Lane Café to Worthing. Much of this path is lined with traditional wooden beach huts. On warm days Goring beach can get very busy and the beachfront café does a roaring trade. It is a short walk into the town centre where you find shops, cafes and a train station.

Sand at low tide overlooked by Rampion Wind Farm.

Around the sixth century Goring became part of the kingdom of Sussex and like in other villages in the south of Sussex, the people of Goring had land to the north that they used as summer pasture in the Weald at Goringlee, near Coolham. This route would have been used as droveways for driving livestock, especially pigs.

The parish of Goring existed at the time of the Domesday survey under the name Garinges. Unlike the other parishes in the area covered by the present Borough of Worthing, which have been in the Rape of Bramber since the eleventh century, Goring forms part of the neighbouring Rape of Arundel. (Rapes are the six ancient subdivisions of the county of Sussex, each named after a castle and its associated town.) The former parish of Goring incorporated four manors. The most important of these passed from the Earls of Arundel to Roger de Montalt, 1st Baron Montalt and several other holders.

The former parish of Goring included Castle Goring, a country house built for Sir Bysshe Shelley, 1st Baronet in the late 1790s. Intermittent residential development began in the nineteenth century and continued throughout the twentieth century. Although the railway came to Goring in 1846 there were so few passengers using Goring Station that it was closed for a period. Goring's population expanded after 1929, when it became part of the Borough of Worthing and again in 1938 when the railway was electrified. Over a period of around fifty years much of old Goring was demolished, although a few buildings survive.

St Mary's church with painting over the chancel arch.   Right: WWI memorial on external south wall.

A church on the present site, dedicated to St Mary was founded in the late twelfth century. It was in regular use for worship thereafter and apart from some additions in the fourteenth century it remained structurally unchanged until the intervention of David Lyon in 1836–1837. Lyon was a rich merchant, who bought land and one of the manor houses in 1834 and set about transforming the area. As well as demolishing the manor house and building Goring Hall, a new mansion, he commissioned architect Decimus Burton to re-design St Mary's church. The twelfth century building was partly demolished and Burton only retained the original arcades in the nave. Lyon paid for the reconstruction himself.

There is a memorial to the casualties of WWI in the form of a sculpture of Jesus which was added to the south exterior wall in the twentieth century. Inside the church one of the first, if not the first, thing you will notice is the painting over the chancel arch. It represents Christ in Glory, 1954 by H. Feibusch. Its strength is its composition with muted colouring but it aroused great controversy and Bishop Bell of Chichester used his authority to override the anticipated reluctance of the Diocesan Chancellor to grant a faculty. Through the churchyard in the Bible garden of the adjoining Parish Office is a bronze statue of Christ by Rosalind Hore 1996 entitled 'Come unto me'.

Now that we have explored these four coastal towns and villages, we are going to move slightly inland, so I will see you at the ruins of Bramber Castle.

Bronze statue of Christ by Rosalind Hore.

CHAPTER 13

BRAMBER

Bramber Castle ruins – gatehouse tower.

Bramber is a former manor village beside the River Adur, north of Shoreham, that is known for its attractions and charm. Located on the northern edge of the South Downs it has Steyning to the west, Upper Beeding to the east but its closest historical connection is with Botolphs to the south. The ecclesiastical parishes of Bramber and Botolphs were united possibly by 1526, but definitely by 1534 with the priest living at Botolphs. Later the priest's official residence became Bramber mansion, now called 'Burletts', on Clay Hill. The union of the civil parish councils came in 1933.

Bramber was a much busier place and served as a port on the Adur but like Steyning, as the river silted up and changed its course it went into decline.

Bramber is most famous for its castle ruins. Built just after the Norman Conquest to help protect King William I's newly won territories; Bramber Castle was the Sussex seat of the Braose family. The castle was part of a network created to guard the strategically important Sussex coast. The region was divided into areas called 'rapes', each protecting a vulnerable point in the coastline, Bramber defended the 'Adur Gap' through the South Downs, where the River Adur flowed to the sea.

Castle ruins.

William de Braose (c1049-1094), who had accompanied Duke William from Normandy, was granted the Rape of Bramber and he built the first castle here in 1073. He also founded the church below the castle and established the Borough of Bramber which grew up along the causeway over the river. The castle remained in the de Braose family's hands for more than two hundred years but with neglect and erosion from the later Middle Ages it fell into ruin. From the seventeenth century the castle became admired for its picturesque beauty.

Not much remains of the original structure as much of the stone was used to construct the bridge and other buildings in the village. In 1966–67 the castle was excavated with another minor survey done in 1987. These indicate that most of it was built between 1073 and 1130. The addition of an outer ditch in 1209 caused the collapse of much of the original curtain wall in the early sixteenth century.

The most prominent feature of the castle that still remains is the gatehouse tower, which still stands to almost its full height; a window and floor joist holes are still visible. Beyond it are the foundations of what is thought to be the living quarters and guardhouse. The original gatehouse appears to have been converted into a single tower at some point in the twelfth century, another 3 metres were added to its height and the entrances were blocked up; this coincides with an increased threat during the reign of King John.

The dressed pillars of an entrance can be identified, but the bulk of the remaining walls now consist of only the rough stone infill. To the north of the gatehouse is the original castle motte (ditch), its earthen mound rising to a height of 30ft (10m). A short distance away is a section of the curtain wall which survives to a height of up to 10ft (3m) in places. The church of St Nicholas beside the ruins was originally built for the castle's inhabitants. During WWII two pillboxes were constructed on the site but have since been removed.

The church of St Nicholas was built in the late eleventh century. It stands on the same mound as Bramber Castle ruins and William de Braose, a close associate of William the Conqueror, built both. Originally it was a cruciform monastic church or chapel for the castle, and it became a parish church in the thirteenth century. The nave with its Norman south doorway and the crossing (now chancel) have survived from the original church; the chancel has Norman carvings on the capitals.

Church of St Nicholas.

St Mary's House.

The tower dates from eighteenth century renovations commissioned by the vicar Thomas Green who died in 1789 and who is commemorated in the church. It is the oldest post-Conquest Norman church in Sussex.

St Mary's House and Gardens is a Grade I listed medieval house which was built in 1470. Its history dates from the days of the Knights Templar when 5 acres of land in Bramber were given to them by the widow of Philip de Braose after his death in 1125. The present building was built c1470 by William of Waynflete, Bishop of Winchester and founder of Magdalen College, Oxford as an inn for pilgrims who were travelling to the tomb of St Thomas of Canterbury.

Sele Priory was a medieval monastic house in Upper Beeding, passed on the associated walk, that has strong ties with the Braose family. In Saxon times Beeding had a near neighbour – the hamlet of Sele. It was a Benedictine priory founded before 1126 and was dedicated to St Peter. It was a dependent priory of the Abbey of St Florent in Saumur in France and was considered an alien priory.

The house was linked with the Braose family from its foundation and continued to receive gifts from family members including the founder of the family William de Braose, his son Philip de Braose and their descendants John de Braose and William de Braose, 1st Baron Braose.

In 1396 the priory became a native religious house, losing all its ties to Saumur except for an annual payment of 11 marks. In 1459 William Waynflete the Bishop of Winchester acquired the patronage of the priory and he incorporated it into his new foundation of Magdalen College, Oxford, although the actual dissolution of the priory did not take place until 1480 when the last monk was pensioned.

Now you can do the associated walk which takes you to Sele Priory, along the banks of the River Adur and on to Bramber Castle ruins and the church of St Nicholas. I will see you back on the coast at Worthing.

St Mary's House plaque by doorway.

SUGGESTED WALK

WALK 16. Sele Priory, River Adur, Bramber Castle ruins, St Nicholas's Church and St Mary's House (7 miles 11.3 km)

Parking. Free car park by the recreation ground. (Post code BN44 3WL.) Although this is a 7 mile walk it is fairly easy as most of it is level walking beside the River Adur but there are a couple of minor climbs near the end; there are eleven stiles to cross some of which could do with a bit of maintenance or be replaced.

Refreshments are available from the Kings Head pub, the Castle Inn or from a village shop at the start / finish.

The Kings Head.

1. Leave the car park and turn right along the High Street using the left-hand pavement. When you are level with the Kings Head pub on the left, go right along Church Lane opposite – signed to St Peters church. (There are a few shops here if you want to buy refreshments for the walk.)

Follow the road past School Road on the right, pass Priory Field on the left, then take the next left which is still a continuation of Church Lane. Go ahead for 40 yards to reach Sele Priory, church of St Peter, on the right.

Sele Priory. Carving above doorway.

Leave the church by the same gate, turn right and continue along the gravel track and in 20 yards go ahead by a 3-way footpath sign. Go down steps, across a bridge and ahead to reach the riverbank of the River Adur. (If you look almost directly ahead just across the river you get a limited view of St Nicholas's church and Bramber Castle ruins which you will be visiting later.)

2. Now turn right and follow the riverbank, soon passing a bridge but you are going to continue for about 2.5 miles to the next bridge, crossing stiles and going through gates as you go. Keep a look out for various birds on the river and numerous butterflies which can just land on the path in front of you. Just follow the riverbank, which can get a little overgrown in a couple of places, until you eventually cross a stile out to the Downs Link path beside a bridge. If you think the bridge looks like an old railway bridge – it is. The Downs Link path largely follows the route of the disused railway line which once ran between Guildford and Shoreham-by-Sea.

Old railway bridge on the Downs Link path.

Peacock butterflies can land in front of you.

3. Go left over the bridge and immediately go left over a stile and walk back along the opposite riverbank – all the way back to the first bridge you passed again crossing stiles and going through gates as you go. After a while if you look over to your left in the distance there is a large isolated building that looks quite insignificant but it is Lancing College which dominates the local skyline and which you will walk past in the next chapter.

As you follow the riverbank path, eventually, you will automatically filter on to an access track. Follow this track for quite some distance but after going through a swing gate the track goes to the right aiming towards a barn – move back over to the left and continue beside the river on the raised grassy bank. Just continue beside the river until you reach the bridge you passed at the start of the river section.

4. At the bridge, turn right before the swing gate, go down the track and go through another swing gate by a 3-way footpath sign. Go left here and follow the grassy path which curves to the right and then to the left. Go through a swing gate and continue along the path, to the rear of houses, until you reach a junction with a marker post on the left.

Remains of curtain wall.

Go ahead up some basic steps, climb a steep bank and continue along a path through trees keeping the old castle motte on your left to reach the main entrance to Bramber Castle ruins on the left.

View along the road.

5. After visiting the ruins, leave by the same entrance and a few yards down the track on your left is the church of St Nicholas. Leave the church via the main lych gate and go left down the path to reach a road. Go left along the road using the right-hand pavement and follow it past the Bramber Castle Inn and the lovely St Mary's House which has historic connections with the Knights Templar; you can visit here if it is open. As you walk down the road look back towards the church and gatehouse tower ruin which proudly overlook the local houses. Continue to cross the river and go ahead along the High Street back to the car park on the left.

CHAPTER 14

WORTHING, LANCING & SHOREHAM-BY-SEA

Worthing beach towards Lancing.

Fishermen on pier with view towards Goring-by-Sea.

WORTHING

Worthing is a large seaside town situated at the foot of the South Downs beside the English Channel. With a current estimated population of 110,000 people and covering an area of 12.5 sq. mi. (32.4 sq. km) the borough is the second largest component of the Brighton/Worthing/Littlehampton Conurbation. Since 2010 northern parts of the borough have formed part of the South Downs National Park and in April 2019 the National Piers Society named Worthing Pier as the Pier of the Year for the second time.

The local area has been populated for at least 6000 years and contains Britain's greatest concentration of Stone Age flint mines, some of which are the earliest mines in Europe. Within the borough the Iron Age hill fort of Cissbury Ring is one of Britain's largest.

Some older local people claim that the name Worthing is derived from a natural annual phenomenon where the seaweed beds off nearby Bognor Regis are ripped up by summer storms and the prevailing Atlantic currents deposit it on Worthing beach. Being a rich source of nitrates, it makes good fertiliser and the decaying weed was sought by farmers from the surrounding area, thus the town could have been known as Wort (weed) -inge (people).

Since c4000BC, the South Downs above Worthing was Britain's earliest and largest flint-mining area with four of the UK's fourteen known flint mines lying within 7 miles (11 km) of the centre of Worthing. An excavation at Little High Street dates the earliest remains from Worthing town centre to the Bronze Age and there is a Bronze Age hill fort on the western fringes of the modern borough at Highdown Hill.

During the Iron Age, one of Britain's largest hill forts was built at Cissbury Ring. The area was part of the civitas of the Regni during the Romano-British period. (The Regni were a civitas [citizens] of Roman Britain, their capital was Noviomagus Reginorum which is known today as Chichester.) Several of the borough's roads date from this time and lie in a grid layout known as a 'centuriation'. A Romano-British farmstead once stood in the centre of the town near the town hall. In the fifth and sixth centuries the area became part of the kingdom of Sussex; the place names of the area including Worthing came from this period.

Worthing remained an agricultural and fishing hamlet for centuries until wealthy visitors started to arrive in the 1750s. Princess Amelia (1783-1810 fifteenth and last child of King George III) stayed in the town in 1798. She was sent to Worthing so that she could bathe in the sea to help her get over tuberculosis as Brighton was considered too racy for the teenage princess. The wealthy continued to stay in Worthing which became a town in 1803. The town grew and elegant developments such as Park Crescent and Liverpool Terrace were begun. In the nineteenth century the area was a stronghold for smugglers and was the site of rioting by the Skeleton Army in the 1880s. (The Skeleton Army was a group that opposed and disrupted The Salvation Army's marches against alcohol in the late nineteenth century).

The Dome cinema on Worthing seafront is one of the oldest cinemas in Britain and is a Grade II listed building owned by PDJ Cinemas Ltd. The cinema has three screens and the name comes from the distinctive dome on top of a three-storey tower over the entrance. It is an Edwardian building, opened in 1911 making it one of the oldest working cinemas in Britain (Brighton's Duke of York's Picture House was opened in 1910). The cinema was opened by Swiss impresario Carl

The Dome cinema.

Adolf Seebold and was originally named The Kursaal, a German word meaning 'cure hall'. The Kursaal was a health centre and entertainment complex used by visitors to Worthing and at the time and it contained the Coronation Hall which was used for roller skating, exhibitions, concerts and events, and the Electric Theatre, the first cinema run for paying audiences in West Sussex. Following the start of WWI leading residents of the town objected to the German name and after a competition with a prize of £1, the cinema was renamed 'The Dome'.

Oscar Wilde (1854–1900) holidayed in Worthing in 1893 and 1894 and on his second visit he wrote *The Importance of Being Earnest*; the

Irish playwright spent two months here initially with his wife Constance and his two sons and they stayed at a house called The Haven. The town has been home to several literary figures in the twentieth century, including Nobel prize winner Harold Pinter (1930–2008).

Liverpool Terrace residences.

Worthing Pier is a Grade II listed pleasure pier designed by Sir Robert Rawlinson that was opened on 12 April 1862. The pier was the thirteenth pier to be built in England at a cost of £6500 and the first pile was driven into the seabed on 4 July 1861. It was originally a promenade deck 960ft (291m) long and 15ft (4.6m) wide. In 1888 it was upgraded to a width of 30ft (9.2m) and the pier head increased to 105ft (32m) for a 650-seat pavilion to be built. It has been named Pier of the Year twice by the National Piers Society in 2006 and 2019. The pier is owned by Worthing Borough Council.

By 1894 a steam ship had begun operating between Worthing Pier and the Chain Pier in Brighton which was 12 miles to the east. Over the Easter weekend of 1894, four-year-old Archie Miles who had become separated from his parents, managed to stow away on board setting off a police hunt; he was reunited with his parents after a night in the workhouse at Brighton and a telegram which was sent to his grandparents in Mayfield. The first moving picture show in Worthing was shown on the pier on 31 August 1896 and is commemorated by a blue plaque.

Worthing Pier.

On Easter Monday in March 1913, the pier was damaged in a storm with gusts blowing at 80 mph. Crowds gathered to watch the pier being battered by the waves; soon after midnight the pier's electricity supply was lost and within minutes the decking between the pavilion and the shore had been washed away. Only the southern end remained, and cut off from the land it was affectionately named 'Easter Island'. A rebuilt pier was opened on 29 May 1914 by the Lord Mayor of London, Sir T. Vansittart Bowater Bart. The Worthing Corporation bought the pier in 1920 for £18,978 and visitors to the pier were charged 2d which included admission to hear an orchestra play in the South Pavilion.

On 10 September 1933 a fire destroyed the Southern Pavilion. Volunteers helped the fire brigade to remove furniture from the burning building and rip up the decking to stop the blaze spreading; the pier was repaired within two years. On its opening the new Southern Pavilion, re-furbished and fully equipped for dance and refreshments was dubbed by the *Daily Mirror* as 'the sun trap of the south'. The central amusement pavilion and the windshield that runs along the length of the pier were built in 1937. The remodelled Streamline Moderne (Art Deco style of architecture) pier is the pier that exists today.

In 1940 the pier was sectioned for fear of German invasion after the British retreat at Dunkirk; army engineers used explosives to blow a 120ft hole in the pier to prevent it being used as a possible landing stage in the event of invasion. In 1942 when fears of invasion had lessened the pier became a recreation centre for troops complete with a canteen, library and billiard tables.

The Worthing Observation Wheel (WOW) is a 46m high wheel with 36 closed gondolas with clear glass. The wheel is the dominant landmark as it towers into the skyline and is the highest wheel in the south of England. The wheel is open daily from 10 a.m. to 10 p.m. seven days a week until 1 October but possibly until 8 November if the weather stays nice. On a clear day there are views up to 10 miles in all directions and at night it is lit up with white lights (that do not flash). The wheel is situated at any one location for the duration of a lease. The lease may be extended or the wheel can be relocated to another location possibly at another site along the West or East Sussex coast.

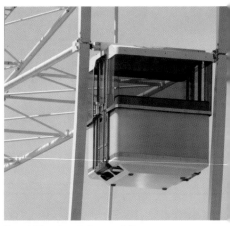

One of 36 enclosed glass gondolas.

Worthing Observation Wheel (WOW).

LANCING

Lancing is technically a village – but a very big village – on the western edge of the Adur Valley. It occupies part of the narrow central section of the Sussex coastal plain between smaller Sompting to the west, Shoreham-by-Sea to the east and the parish of Coombes to the north. Most of Lancing is a large sprawl of housing which is a result of the massive in-filling of the Sussex coast after WWII. It is a mix of mid-rise coastal urban homes and farms with wildlife reserves on the northern chalk downs.

Like most West Sussex beaches South Lancing beach is shingle with compacted wet sand exposed when the tide is out. At the top of the beach there are coloured beach huts and there are plenty of cafés, bars and shops in the area. To welcome visitors to Lancing there is a boat on the beach which at the time of writing had a flag thanking the NHS for their work during the COVID-19 epidemic. With permission from the local council the local bandstand was re-painted by the Worthing Ward with the help of full-time missionaries; the new design illustrates 'conflict leading to a brighter dawn'.

Lancing beach towards Shoreham-by-Sea.

In the mid-nineteenth century the village was a popular seaside resort that gained favour from the gentry of the time for its secluded atmosphere but it has just about kept its identity separate from its bigger neighbours Worthing and Shoreham-by-Sea. Shoreham Airport has actually done the most to help prevent Lancing being swallowed up by the megalopolis of the Sussex coast as it takes up a large area of grassland near the Adur's west bank. Much of Lancing's northern boundary runs along the Ladywell Stream, a tributary of the River Adur which runs from the South Downs near to Lancing College. The source of the Ladywell Stream, the Ladywell Spring, is believed to be an ancient holy well or sacred stream with pre-Christian significance.

In the Middle Ages the parish of Lancing had three settlements – North Lancing, South Lancing and Pende. Pende was a small port alongside the River Adur but changes in the course of the river and the Teville Stream meant most traces of Pende were lost by the seventeenth century.

Widewater Lagoon Local Nature Reserve is a long and narrow brackish lagoon and the only known location of the probably extinct Ivell's sea anemone.

Immediately to the north of Lancing is Lancing Ring a name given to a small hill which rises to 109 metres above sea level. It is a Nature Reserve in the South Downs National Park which we pass on the associated walk. Lancing Ring is

Bandstand representing – 'conflict leading to a brighter dawn'.

Welcome to Lancing boat on beach.

protected by its designation as an Area of Outstanding Natural Beauty. It is owned and managed by Adur District Council but it is looked after by the volunteer group Friends of Lancing Ring. It gets its name because a ring of beeches was planted in the late eighteenth century that was inspired by the nearby Cissbury Ring. Many of the trees were blown down in the 1987 storm but many have been replanted, some as recently as 2012 to mark the Queen's Diamond Jubilee.

Lancing Ring covers 73 acres (29.4 hectares) and the chalk grassland is notable for butterflies, adders and common lizards. There is deciduous woodland with wild flowers including early purple orchids, and a dew pond which attracts dragonflies such as the broad-bodied chaser and numerous newts.

Lancing College is an independent boarding and day school located in the South Downs Area of Outstanding Natural Beauty. It was founded in 1848 by Nathaniel Woodard and teaches around 600 pupils aged 13 to 18; originally for boys, girls were admitted in 1970. The college dominates the landscape and can be seen from miles around; it overlooks the River Adur and the Ladywell Stream. Lancing was the first of more than thirty schools founded by Woodard and others in Sussex include Ardingly College and Hurstpierpoint College. Around 65% of pupils are boarders at a cost of £37,065 per year and 35% are day pupils at a cost of £25,320 per year (in 2020).

The foundation stone of the chapel was laid in 1868 but the chapel was not completed before Woodard's death, and in fact it remains unfinished. It is 50 metres high with foundations going down 20 metres into the ground but the original plans were for a tower at the west end which would have made it 100 metres high. The apex of the vaulting rises to 27.4 metres; it was designed by R.H. Carpenter and William Slater using sandstone from Scaynes Hill near Haywards Heath.

The chapel was dedicated to St Mary and St Nicholas in 1911 although the college worshipped in the finished crypt from 1875. Inside is the tomb of the founder, three organs and a rose window designed by Stephen Dykes Bower completed in 1977 which is the largest rose window in England at 32ft (9.75m) in diameter. The eastern organ is a two-manual mechanical organ built by Danish firm Frobenius and was installed and voiced in situ in 1986; also, that year saw the completion of the rebuild of the four-manual Walker organ at the west end of the chapel. A stained-glass window commissioned in memory of Trevor Huddleston OL, was consecrated by Archbishop Desmond Tutu on 22 May 2007.

Pevsner described Lancing College Chapel as 'some atonement for the many heaps of ugliness which the nineteenth century unloaded blindly on the English landscape'. The Writer Evelyn Waugh and lyricist Sir Tim Rice attended Lancing College. The chapel is closed to the public.

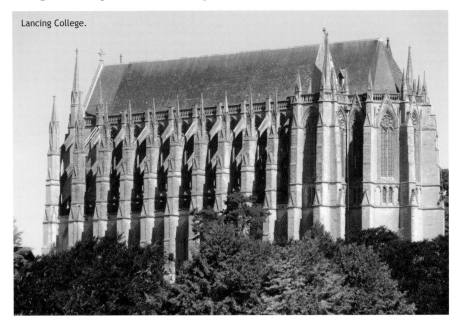

Lancing College.

SHOREHAM-BY-SEA

Shoreham-by-Sea is a seaside town and port that is bordered in the north by the South Downs, Lancing to the east and to its west by the Adur Valley. It is dominated by its port facilities and the chimney of Shoreham Power Station (actually in Southwick but described under Shoreham) is dominant and can be seen from all along the Sussex coast and for miles out to sea. The port is busy and its surrounding area is packed with warehousing and industrial properties.

Shoreham beach lies to the west of the harbour where the River Adur enters the sea, it has a slope which is quite steep in places and consists of shingle with exposed wet sand when the tide is out. Before WWII a Bungalow Town sprang up on Shoreham Beach with many theatre and film folk residing in the upmarket coastal shanty town. Security fears during the war led to the clearance of many of the cabins on the beach and the rebuilding after the war was done on a more permanent scale.

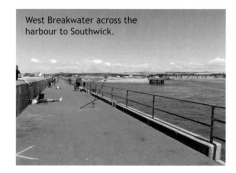

West Breakwater across the harbour to Southwick.

Old Shoreham Toll Bridge.

Old Shoreham dates to pre-Roman times. The church of St Nicholas by the River Adur is partly Anglo-Saxon and the name of the town has an Old English origin. The town and port of New Shoreham was established by the Norman conquerors at the end of the eleventh century.

Old Shoreham Toll Bridge is a bridge crossing over the River Adur and was the last public road toll bridge in Sussex at the time of its closure to road traffic in 1970. The Old Shoreham Toll Bridge was built to cross the River Adur between Shoreham and Lancing. Before it was built in 1781 the River Adur was an obstacle for east-west travel along the coastal plain of southern England. Travellers had the choice and could travel miles inland to cross the bridge at Bramber, to ford the river on horseback or to use the ferry that operated where the bridge is now.

In 2008 the bridge had major

Adur Ferry Bridge at Shoreham-on-Sea.

Rotating centre section.

refurbishment with the aim of extending its life by another thirty years. It is now a designated bridleway and a popular landmark used by foot, bicycle and horseback (you will cross it on the associated walk). The refurbishment replaced the pile head crossbeams, deck support longitudinal beams and handrails as well as selective replacement of components of each of the 27 pile bents. The bridge was re-opened by HRH The Duke of York on 23 October 2008 and the bridge was listed at Grade II by English Heritage on 12 October 1954.

The Adur Ferry Bridge is an opening bridge that crosses the tidal River Adur and salt marsh at Shoreham-by-Sea that replaced a 1920s narrow concrete footbridge. A bridge was required for both pedestrians and cyclists that needed to be a landmark and which was capable of opening up the river for better access for boats.

Environmental factors had to be considered such as wintering wildfowl and it was suggested that the design incorporate high glass for some protection from the wind. The chosen design was a swing bridge featuring a central section supported by a mast and cable-stay. The 50 metre platform section rests on a mechanism in the central concrete pier of the bridge that can rotate to an open position in three minutes to allow boats to pass. The swing bridge mechanism can accommodate a tidal range of up to 7 metres. Materials for the bridge were transported by barge to minimise disruption during construction and the design features low energy lighting on the handrails.

The Adur Ferry Bridge was opened in November 2013 by HRH the Duke of Gloucester. It took 72,000-man hours to complete and weighs approximately 700 tonnes.

Shoreham Redoubt (Shoreham Fort) is a defensive structure at the entrance to Shoreham Harbour at the mouth of the River Adur. It was completed in June 1857 for fear of a possible French invasion at a cost of £11,685. The fort consisted of a gun platform 15ft (4.6m) above sea level and was in the shape of a lunette (straight sided crescent). The gun platform and ramparts were surrounded by a ditch with a Carnot Wall (a type of loop-holed wall built in the ditch of a fort) running along its centre, which was designed to halt attackers attempting to cross the ditch. Instead of open bastions Shoreham had a caponier (a type of defensive structure in a fort – from the French

Shoreham Redoubt (Shoreham Fort).

caponnière, meaning 'chicken coup') with a brick roof at each of the three angles of the walls so riflemen could fire along the walls at besiegers in the ditch. The central caponier straddled the ditch and was connected to the fort by a tunnel under the gun platform and ramparts. The barrack block at the rear had room for 38 men and the fort was armed with six 68-pounder guns on traversing platforms.

Shoreham Power Station (actually in Southwick) is a 420MWe (Megawatts electric) combined cycle gas-fired power station that was built on the site of the Brighton B Power Station. One of Scottish Power's four Combined Cycle Gas Turbine (CCGT) stations Shoreham operates at various loads in order to meet the energy needs of 400,00 homes on the south coast. It uses a gas turbine, and a steam turbine and generator to provide one of the more efficient forms of thermal generation. It was opened in 2000 and operated as a fifty-fifty joint venture between Scottish Power and

Shoreham Power Plant (Southwick).

AEP. The plant was fully acquired by Scottish Power in the autumn of 2004.

Its location at Shoreham Harbour has a history of electricity production and the site was formerly occupied by the Brighton B Power Station. The new modern station used several features from the old plant such as a cable tunnel under the harbour and cooling water outfall, and Shoreham's 106 metre chimney – the tallest structure in West Sussex – is on the same site as the old brick stack that was demolished in 1998.

A main advantage of modern CCGTs is their efficiency at converting fuel into electrical energy which is typically around 55%. This means less fuel consumption and lower levels of emissions per unit of electricity generated compared with conventional thermal stations. Burning natural gas gives rise to minimal emissions of dust, ash or sulphur dioxide which has been linked with 'acid rain' damage to ecosystems and respiratory irritation in people.

Brighton City Airport (Shoreham Airport) was founded in 1910 and is the oldest airport in the UK and the oldest purpose-built commercial airport in the world. It is now owned by Brighton City Airport Ltd (BCAL) and the 1930s' Art Deco terminal building designed by R Stayers Hessell Tiltman is a Grade II listed building. It has a CAA Public Use Aerodrome Licence that allows flights for the public, transport of passengers or for flying instruction. Flying started at Shoreham in 1911 which is just nine years after the Wright Brother's maiden flight. The airport was famous for the annual Shoreham Air Show.

The first aviator to fly here was Harold H. Piffard in 1910; a memorial garden celebrates his flight. The aerodrome was officially opened on 20 June 1911 and the first flying school opened in 1913.

The airport is used by privately owned light aeroplanes, flying schools and for light aircraft and helicopter maintenance and sales. A number of operators provide flying lessons, sight-seeing and pleasure flights, including the experience of flying in two T-6 Harvard WWII training aircraft. On 2 May 2014 Brighton City Airport

Ltd took ownership of the airport and its operations and the airport was officially renamed as Brighton City (Shoreham) Airport.

The airport used to host the Royal Air Forces Association (RAFA) Shoreham Air Show for around twenty-five years but on the 22 August 2015, a Hawker Hunter, jet fighter crashed on to the A27 sadly killing eleven people and the show has not been held since.

The River Adur gives its name to the Adur district of West Sussex. It is 20 miles (32Km) long and was once navigable for large ships up as far as Steyning where there was a large Saxon port, but by the eleventh century the lower river became silted up and the port moved down to deeper waters at the mouth of the river in Shoreham-by-Sea.

The Adur begins as two separate branches, the western Adur and the eastern Adur, which meet 2 km west

Brighton City (Shoreham) Airport.

of Henfield. The western Adur rises at Slinfold and is tidal as far north as Bines Bridge near Bines Green, south of West Grinstead. The eastern Adur rises at Ditchling Common in East Sussex from where it crosses into West Sussex and meets Herrings Stream at Twineham. At Shermanbury the eastern Adur is fed by the Cowfold Stream. The normal tidal limit is just below this at the footbridge near Shermanbury church although a weir just above the confluence with the western Adur means that only the highest tides reach here. Up until the early 1800s boats could navigate to Mock Bridge where the A281 crosses the Adur.

The two branches of the river meet west of Henfield before flowing between Upper Beeding and Bramber past Coombes, through a gap in the South Downs near Lancing College where the Adur is fed by the Ladywell Stream. It continues to reach the English Channel at Shoreham-by-Sea. The mouth of the Adur is now 2 miles (3km) from the town centre of Shoreham due to longshore drift (a geological process that consists of the transportation of sediments). Previously, the river mouth was further east in Portslade but an opening in the sea was made which allowed the creation of Southwick Ship Canal.

Now try and do the associated walk which is the most difficult in this book but you will be rewarded with lovely views. I will see you in Chapter 15 where we explore a more industrialised section of the West Sussex coast but which hides some unexpected gems.

SUGGESTED WALK

WALK 17. Lancing College, views and the River Adur (10.0 miles 16.1 km)

Parking. There is roadside parking in St Nicholas Lane by the church (Post code BN43 5NH). This is the hardest, most strenuous and longest walk in this book. It is a popular walk with people of various ages but the first half of it involves a long steady, sweeping climb up on to the South Downs Way which is demanding. The walk takes you past Lancing College and Lancing Ring Nature Reserve, there are views throughout towards Shoreham and Worthing and there is a total of 3 miles of walking beside the River Adur. Remember to take a drink and a cap if it is a hot day. Refreshments are available at the Amsterdam Inn at the start/finish.

1. From St Nicholas Lane, pass the church on your right and go ahead to the main road. Cross the road and go almost directly ahead along the concrete path to reach the Old Shoreham Toll Bridge. Cross the bridge with your first view of the college in front of you and Shoreham Airport away to your left; throughout this walk you will see light aircraft above you that have just taken off or are coming in to land. On the far side of the bridge

St Nicholas church.

go immediately right along the path with the River Adur on your right. (I have purposely taken you this way so that you can walk a short distance along the river looking upstream.)

Pass beneath the A27 and continue (ahead of you is the chimney at Shoreham old cement works that will be in view throughout much of this walk and which you will pass near the end of the walk when you are returning beside the river). Just after you pass an isolated building on your left, Creek Cottage, the path goes left to a small parking area by a road (Coombes Road). Go left along the road and follow it until you reach a road on your right signed to Lancing College. Go up the road and in a short distance go right into the grounds of the college by an access road and footpath sign that is beside a stile.

2. Go up the access road and just as it descends go left at a marker post. Go through a swing gate and steadily climb a track with glimpses of the college on the right through the trees. (As you climb look back on your left for views of Shoreham Airport, bridge, Rampion Wind Farm and Power Station). At the end of the path you reach a lane by a 3-way footpath sign. Go right and continue climbing up the quiet lane which soon becomes a track and continues up between trees.

140

Lancing College through the trees.

Sign for Lancing Ring Nature Reserve.

At a junction go right and continue climbing passing a sign for Lancing Ring Local Nature Reserve on the left (partially obscured by growth). Pass a small car park on the left and continue to the right of a metal gate. When the path opens out continue ahead with good views of Worthing to your left. Now just follow the path, enjoying the views, and climb the hill in front of you. (you have views of the cement works away to your right and there is also an isolated building in front of you / slightly right – just keep going). Eventually you arrive at a junction by a 3-way footpath sign with an electric pylon beside you on the right. Continue ahead still climbing gently and go through a swing gate to the left of a metal gate and continue. Go through a wide metal gate and continue ahead and in a short distance you reach Bostal Road, not signed, by a gravel parking area. Turn right along the road for 30 yards using the raised grass path to reach a 3-way footpath sign.

3. Go right through a swing gate (South Downs Way) and follow the field edge path with a wire fence on your left. At the gate you will have noticed that the South Downs Way also continued ahead. If you had followed it ahead you would have eventually reached Chanctonbury Ring on the South Downs Way and Cissbury Ring is away to the west. Just follow this path aiming for the aerials on the hill ahead – don't worry, you are not going to them. Go through a swing gate

and continue passing an unexpected pig farm beside you on your right. Go through another swing gate and ahead down a right-hand field edge. At a farm track continue downhill with the wire fence on your right. Go through a swing gate to the right of a wide metal gate and go down a track beneath trees. The track bends left by a marker post and you continue for a short distance to reach a road.

Pig beside pathway.

Go right down the road and about 40 yards after passing a sign for Botolphs (by the entrance to Pear Tree Cottage on the left) go left through a swing gate and follow a left field edge. In the far corner, cross a sleeper bridge and go right along a gravel track. At a 4-way footpath sign go left to reach the bank of the River Adur by a 3-way footpath sign.

River Adur.

4. Now go right and just follow the meandering right hand river bank, soon passing a bridge and the old cement works that you have seen throughout this walk. (It is only now that you can see what an absolute eyesore this site is, but it is a well-known local landmark.) Keep a look out for the varied birdlife on the river (on the day I did this walk there were two cormorants diving down into the river to feed but I was too slow to photograph them properly – or they were too fast?) and you also get a different view of Lancing College. Eventually you arrive back at the section of river you walked at the start. Walk around the spur, through the car park and then continue beside the river on the other side.

Go back under the A27 and over on your left you will see the top of the church where you parked. Re-cross the Old Shoreham Toll Bridge, cross the main road and go along the road opposite, behind the bus shelter back to the church. The Amsterdam Inn is awaiting you if you need refreshments and a well-deserved rest.

River Adur and Lancing College.

Cormorant.

142

CHAPTER 15

SOUTHWICK & PORTSLADE-BY-SEA

Southwick Lock.

Boat at Shoreham Canal in Portslade.

SOUTHWICK

Southwick is a small town in the Adur district of West Sussex that borders Shoreham-by-Sea and shares the east arm of Shoreham Harbour. Driving along the A259 you could be forgiven for thinking that Southwick is just a sprawl of industries and warehouses but you would be wrong.

The town is loosely divided into three sections. South of the A259 is the harbour with industries and warehouses; north of the A259 up to the Old Shoreham Road is mainly residential properties that date from the middle of the nineteenth century to the 1950s; and north of the Old Shoreham Road to the South Downs are newer residences. Its Saxon name was Esmerewick, meaning east pool hamlet and in 1309 it was first recorded as Suthewicke.

Beach towards Shoreham Harbour.

Southwick beach lies to the east of Shoreham Harbour, where the River Adur enters the sea. Again, it is mainly shingle with exposed wet sand when the tide is out. The beach has a gentle slope and is intersected by a number of wooden groynes. Behind the beach is a promenade with the very popular Carats Café.

The town grew as the area became popular as a holiday destination with many of the properties being tourist accommodation. On 12 May 1840 the railway arrived which added to the popularity of the area.

A Roman villa from the first century AD stood on the site now occupied by the Southwick Methodist Church at the junction of Manor Hall Road and Southwick Street. It was one of the most important villas in Sussex that was elaborately decorated and similar in design to Fishbourne Roman Villa. The villa has a permanent exhibition about its history and the various efforts to excavate it in the Manor Cottage Heritage Centre.

Kings Cottages on Southwick Green is reputed to be where King Charles II stayed overnight before escaping to France from the fishing village of Brighthelmstone (Brighton).

The Southwick Ship Canal branches off from the estuary of the River Adur. It is 1.75 miles long and runs east-west parallel with the shoreline, providing facilities with Shoreham. The canal was once the river channel, but the mouth of the river has been moved to the west enabling its former bed to be used for the canal.

This area has a long history as a centre for shipping. Southwick is a Saxon name that was given to the town by Saxons who landed at the river mouth. In Norman times the port was used for importing wine and exporting wool. King John landed here in 1199 and it became a Royal Arsenal. A shipbuilding industry developed and in 1346 Shoreham supplied 26 ships to Edward III for his wars with the French.

Entrance to harbour between east and west breakwaters.

Walkway over lock.

The mouth of the river was not ideal for shipping as large amounts of shingle moved with the tides so in 1760 the Commissioners of Shoreham Harbour met to plan a new entrance to the river further to the west. In 1816 a second channel was cut through the shingle bank at the site of the present river mouth. This left 1.75 miles (2.82 km) of former river bed. The old channel became the Southwick Ship Canal which was first used by shipping in 1855. A gas works was built between the canal and the sea in 1870 and a power station was built in 1897, both needed supplies of coal which arrived on the canal for offloading at wharfs.

Improvements have been made to the canal. The bed was dredged to make it deeper and a new lock, the Prince George Lock, was completed in 1933. The lock was 170.5 feet (52m) long, 18 feet (5.5m) wide and can accommodate ships with a draught (vertical distance between waterline and bottom of the hull) of 18 feet (5.5m). In 1944 the port was used as a departure point for troops for the D-Day landings. Trade increased when a second coal-fired power station was commissioned in 1953. In 1957 the entrance from the sea was improved by the addition of east and west breakwaters (which you can walk along for lovely views of Shoreham Harbour and the coastlines) and in 1958 Prince Phillip opened an additional lock which carries his name. This lock is considerably bigger than the Prince George Lock at 374ft (114m) long, 57ft (17m) wide and suitable for draughts up to 22ft (6.7m). This lock is mainly used for commercial vessels whilst the smaller lock is used for fishing boats and yachts.

In 2015 planning permission was granted for two Norvento nED100 wind turbines to be located in Southwick near the east breakwater. They were erected in 2016 and in an average year the two turbines produce an annual average of 555,000 kWh of electricity, matching the energy demand of the port's pump house that they are connected to. Both wind and solar power play a big part in the port's energy strategy. The Shoreham Power Station with its 106m tall chimney was described in Chapter 14 under Shoreham-by-Sea.

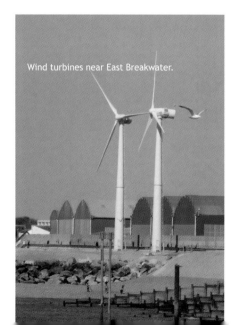
Wind turbines near East Breakwater.

PORTSLADE-BY-SEA

Portslade is a village and a western suburb of the city of Brighton and Hove. The original settlement was Portslade Village which is a mile inland to the north that was built up in the sixteenth century. With the arrival of the railway from Brighton in 1840 it encouraged rapid development of the coastal area and in 1896 the southern part, formerly known as Copperas Gap, was granted urban district status and renamed Portslade-by-Sea, making it distinct from Portslade Village. Portslade is actually the boundary town between West Sussex and East Sussex and the dividing line is a footpath that extends from the seafront up on to the South Downs.

Portslade Village nestles in the valley of the South Downs and still retains its rural charm with flint buildings, a village green and St Nicholas church which dates from c1150. Portslade-by-Sea straddles the small but busy seaport harbour basin of Shoreham Harbour along its east arm and is the industrial centre of Brighton and Hove.

Portslade beach towards Brighton and Hove.

A notable building in Portslade Village is Portslade Manor, one of the few surviving ruins of a Norman manor; built in the twelfth century it is now a Scheduled Ancient Monument. The Old Shoreham Road is thought to form part of the Chichester (Noviomagus Reginorum) to Portslade Roman road and Roman remains and a Roman burial site were found in Roman Road. The old name for Portslade-by-Sea, Copperas Gap, suggests that the coast was used for the production of copperas or green vitriol which is a form of ferrous sulphate used in the textile industry. The process took more than six years and made use of iron pyrite-rich nodules that could be found in the strata of Sussex greensand stone that emerges at this point in the coast.

Now I will see you at our final stop – Brighton and Hove. Although in East Sussex I am including Brighton as it is a large city with many attractions and I want to share it across this West Sussex Coast book and a future East Sussex Coast book.

Boats at the canal (Shoreham Harbour).

CHAPTER 16

HOVE & BRIGHTON

Palace Pier Brighton.

Architecture in Adelaide Crescent, Hove.

Brighton is a constituent part of the city of Brighton and Hove which were previously separate towns. It was in 1997 that the town of Brighton and its neighbouring town Hove were joined to form the unitary authority of Brighton and Hove, which was granted city status by Queen Elizabeth II as part of the millennium celebrations in 2000. Geographically the city of Brighton and Hove is considered part of East Sussex and it is referred to as such for postal addresses. However, in local authority terms East and West Sussex are separately run counties and Brighton and Hove is independent of them both as a unitary authority responsible for all its local government services. The Local Authority boundary for Brighton and Hove is between Portslade and Saltdean along the south coast. It is for this reason that I am including Brighton and Hove at the end of this book and will hopefully be starting with it in an East Sussex Coast book; as there is so much to see and so much to describe, I can split it across the two books.

The beach at Brighton and Hove (from here just referred to as Brighton) is very famous and very popular with holidaymakers and day-trippers as Brighton train station is on a main line to London with all the intermediary stations on route making easy to travel to. The beaches is comprised of pebbles interspersed with regular groynes. To the rear of the beach there is a popular cycle lane and Hove Lawns is a grassy area with many facilities along the Hove section as well as plenty of beach huts. Brighton has the cycle lane but the beach is overlooked mainly by hotels such as the Grand Hotel and the Hilton Metropole.

Hove seafront towards Portslade.

Brighton and Hove bandstand.

Hove was originally a small but ancient fishing village that was surrounded by farmland but it grew rapidly in the nineteenth century in response to the development of Brighton. By the Victorian era it was a fully developed town. Old spellings of Hove include Hou (Domesday Book), la Houue (1288), Huua (thirteenth century), Houve (thirteenth and fourteenth centuries), Huve (fourteenth and fifteenth centuries), Hova (sixteenth century) and Hoova (1675). No other place in Britain is called Hove and single-syllable names as a whole are rare in Sussex.

Fossilised remains from the Pleistocene era have been found in three locations in Hove. An 11lb 2oz (5kg) molar from *elephas antiguus* was excavated from the garden of a house in Poplar Avenue, teeth from a juvenile elephant were found deep in the soil at Ventnor Villas and a prehistoric horse's tooth was found in the soil near Hove Street. During building work near Palmeira Square in 1856-57, workmen levelled a substantial burial mound; a prominent feature of the landscape since 1200 BC, the 20ft (6.1m) high tumulus yielded the Hove amber cup. Made of translucent red Baltic amber and about the same size as a regular china tea cup, the artefact is displayed in the Hove Museum and Art Gallery. Also buried in the coffin in which the amber cup was found were a stone battle-axe, a whetstone and a bronze dagger whose appearance is characteristic of the Wessex culture.

Grand Hotel.

Hilton Metropole Hotel.

A well-known reply by residents of Hove, usually humorous, when asked if they live in Brighton is 'Hove, actually' thus maintaining a distinction with their less genteel neighbour. In the 1990s the Hove Borough Council used the slogan 'Hove, actually' to promote the town for tourism.

There is archaeological evidence of a settlement at Brighton that dates back to the Bronze Age, Roman and Anglo-Saxon periods. The ancient settlement of Brighthelmstone was documented in the Domesday Book (1086). The town's importance grew in the Middle Ages as the Old Town developed but it languished in the early modern period, affected by foreign attacks, storms, a suffering economy and a declining population. Brighton started to attract more visitors following improved road transport to London and after becoming a boarding point for boats sailing to France; it also became popular as a health resort for bathing as a purported cure for illnesses.

In Georgian times Brighton developed as a fashionable seaside resort which was encouraged by the patronage of the Prince Regent, later King George IV, who spent much time in the town and constructed the Royal Pavilion in the Regency era. Brighton continued to grow following the arrival of the railways in 1841. Many of the major attractions were built in the Victorian era including the Grand Hotel, the Hilton Metropole, the Palace Pier and the West Pier. The town continued to grow into the twentieth century expanding to incorporate more areas within the town's boundaries before joining with Hove.

The West Pier was designed by Eugenius Birch and opened in 1866. It was the first pier to be Grade I listed in Britain but has become derelict since its closure in 1975. It was built during a boom in pleasure pier building and was designed to attract tourists. It was extended in 1893 and a concert hall was added in 1916. During this time, it reached its peak attendance with two million visitors between 1918-19. Its popularity declined after WWII and concerts were replaced with a funfair and tearoom. A local company took ownership in 1965 but could not meet the increased maintenance costs and ultimately filed for bankruptcy. They could not find a suitable buyer so the pier closed in 1975 and subsequently fell into disrepair. The pier gradually collapsed during the early twenty-first century. Major sections collapsed in late 2002 and two fires in March and May 2003 left little of the original structure and English Heritage declared it beyond repair. Structured demolition took place in 2010 to make way for the i360 observation tower and further storm damage has occurred since.

West Pier January 2004.

British Airways i360.

The British Airways i360 is located on Brighton seafront by what is left of the West Pier. The 450ft viewing tower is a local landmark and can be seen from miles around. The experience takes you 450ft up in a futuristic glass viewing pod which was conceived and designed by Marks Barfield Architects who were the creators of the London Eye. From the top there are views across the city to the South Downs National Park and on a clear day to the Isle of Wight, 49 miles away. The glass viewing pod is fully enclosed and spacious, it is ten times the size of a London Eye capsule. There is room for 175 visitors to stand at the edge of the pod and look out or to move around for a different view. The Sky Bar on board the pod serves Nyetimber sparkling wine and other drinks from Sussex. At the end of the flight the pod descends into the beach building.

Brighton Palace Pier.

The Brighton Palace Pier, which is more commonly known as Brighton Pier or Palace Pier is a Grade II listed pleasure pier. It opened in 1899 and was the third pier in Brighton after the Royal Suspension Chain Pier and the West Pier but now, it is the only one left in operation. The pier quickly became popular and had become a frequently-visited theatre and entertainment venue by 1911. Apart from closures due to wars, it continued to hold regular entertainment up to the 1970s. The theatre was damaged in 1973 and following a buy-out was removed in 1986. This changed the pier's character from seaside entertainment to an amusement

Royal Pavilion.

park with various fairground rides and roller coasters. The pier is still popular with the public and had over four million visitors in 2016. It has featured in many works of British culture, including the gangster thriller *Brighton Rock*, the comedy *Carry On at Your Convenience* and the Who's concept album and film *Quadrophenia*.

The Royal Pavilion which is also known as the Brighton Pavilion is a Grade I listed former Royal residence. Beginning in 1787, it was built in three stages as a seaside retreat for George, Prince of Wales, who became Prince Regent in 1811 and King George IV in 1820. It is built in the Indo-Saracenic style prevalent in India for most of the nineteenth century. The current appearance of the Pavilion, with its domes and minarets is the work of architect John Nash who extended the building starting in 1815. George IV's successors William IV and Victoria also used the Pavilion but Queen Victoria decided that Osborne House on the Isle of Wight should be the royal seaside retreat and the Pavilion was sold to the town of Brighton in 1850. On 1 April 2020 management and operation of the Royal Pavilion & Museums' buildings and collections were transferred from Brighton and Hove City Council to a new charity – the Royal Pavilion and Museums Trust (RPMT). The purchase of the Royal Pavilion from Queen Victoria marked the beginnings of the site's attraction as a tourist destination. The Royal Pavilion has been changed from a private residence to a public attraction under civic ownership and around 400,000 people visit annually.

About 6 miles north of Brighton is Clayton railway tunnel and for many it represents the arrival at Brighton after travelling from any of the stations from London. Clayton railway tunnel is the longest tunnel (1.25 miles) on the London to Brighton railway line; it begins in Clayton and runs up to 270 feet (82 metres) below ground. The tunnel was built in the 1840s costing £90,000. The farmer who owned the land would not grant access to the tunnel unless an edifice was built at its entrance and so the railway company built a castellated entrance around the tunnel which still exists. In 1861 there was a collision at Clayton Tunnel between two trains killing 25 people and injuring 176 others. Clayton Tunnel is passed on walk 19.

Close to Clayton Tunnel are the very popular Clayton Windmills which are known locally as Jack and Jill which stand on the South Downs above the village of Clayton and are Grade II listed buildings.

Jill (white) is a post mill originally built in Dyke Road in 1821. She was known as Lashmar's New Mill and replaced Lashmar's Old Mill. In 1830, the windshaft broke, causing the sails to crash to the ground. Lashmar's New Mill was the most southerly of the three Dyke Road post mills. In 1852 she was moved to Clayton by a team of horses and oxen. The working life of the mills came to an end in 1906 and in 1908 Jill was damaged in a storm. She lost her fantail and sails over the years until in 1953 restoration was carried out by E. Hole and Son, the Burgess Hill millwrights, funded by Cuckfield Rural District Council. In 1978, restoration of Jill to working order commenced and she ground flour again in 1986. During the Great Storm of 1987, the mill's sails were set in motion whilst the brake was still on, setting fire to the mill. Some members of the Windmill Society were able to get to the mill and were able to save her. Today, Jill is in working order and is open to the public most Sundays

Clayton tunnel.

Jill windmill June 2020.

between May and September. Occasionally, she produces stoneground wholemeal flour the vast majority of which is sold to visitors. It is ground from organic wheat that is grown locally in Sussex. When the wind is blowing and Jill is in operation there is a guide available to explain the process of milling. Jill is owned by Mid Sussex District Council.

Duncton Mill was built in 1765. It was owned by Viscount Montague and leased for ninety-nine years. It was demolished in 1866, leaving the roundhouse to be used as a store. It was a post mill with a single storey roundhouse and four common sails and had two pairs of millstones. The head wheel from Duncton Mill was used as the brake wheel in Jack when that mill was built.

Jack (black) is a five-storey tower mill built in 1866 to replace Duncton Mill. Worked as a pair with Jill, Jack worked until c1907. Unusually, Jack mill has a male name whereas almost every other mill in the country is considered female. In 1928, while a pit was being dug for a water tank, an Anglo-Saxon skeleton was discovered that was later removed to the British Museum. Jack is in private ownership and is not open to the public. Compared to Jill, Jack does look a bit sorry for himself and is best seen in late autumn when the leaves have fallen off the surrounding trees which obscure him. The windmills are visited on Walk 19.

Devil's Dyke a 100m deep V-shaped valley.

Devil's Dyke is a 100m deep V-shaped valley on the South Downs Way near Brighton. The Dyke is formed in rocks of the chalk group which originated as marine sediments during the Cretaceous period. The 300ft deep valley was carved by tremendous amounts of water running off the Downs during the last Ice Age when large amounts of snow thawed and the frozen chalk prevented any further absorption; erosion was aided by the freeze-thaw cycle and the valley was deepened by the 'sludging' of the saturated chalk.

Local folklore explains the valley as being the work of the devil. The legend says that the devil was digging a trench to allow the sea to flood the many churches in the Weald of Sussex. The digging disturbed an old woman who lit a candle, or angered a rooster causing it to crow, making the devil believe the morning was fast approaching. The devil then fled, leaving his trench unfinished.

Another legend says that rather than digging to flood Sussex, he was simply in a huge goat-like form intending to crush the surrounding area. He smelt the tang of salt water in the wind and fearing his coat would get damp (for he is vain to the point of sin) he fled leaving nothing but a hoof-print, now known as Devil's Dyke. You can walk around Devil's Dyke on Walk 18.

Now we are at the end of our West Sussex Coast journey and all that remains is for you to do Walk 18 at Devil's Dyke and Walk 19 to see Clayton train tunnel and Jack and Jill windmills. Walk 20 is a very basic walk around the City of Brighton so that you can do a simple route which passes as many attractions as possible. I hope to see you for a journey along the East Sussex coast in the near future.

SUGGESTED WALK

WALK 18. Devil's Dyke (3.25 miles 5.2 km)

Parking. There is roadside parking by the Royal Oak pub in Poynings. (Post code BN45 7AQ.) This is a hilly walk with a couple of long and very steep climbs. There are five stiles and over 100 steps to contend with. Refreshments are available from the Royal Oak and Devil's Dyke pubs.

The Royal Oak.

1. With your back to the pub, go left down the road using the raised left-hand pavement. (If you look carefully at the name of the pub in the photo you may see what you think is a major spelling mistake. The pubs name is ORAL OKAY. This is deliberate and relates to the time of lockdown due to COVID 19 and it is saying that it's good to talk – ORAL OKAY is an anagram of ROYAL OAK.) Soon you pass an old-fashioned-style garage on the right-hand side but for now you continue along the raised path to its end. At its end you arrive beside a conical-roofed memorial called Cora's Corner, which is a tribute to a former resident of Poynings. Cora was the wife of impresario Emile Littler and they lived at Downmere in Poynings for many years. Cora died in 2004 aged 102 and the benches are named after her daughters - Judy's seat and Merrilee's seat. Opposite the shelter is the Holy Trinity church.

Cora's Corner Memorial.

From Cora's Corner return back along the raised path and when you reach The Forge garage on the left, cross over and walk along the left side of it with a stream on your left. Enter a field at the rear of the garage via a stile in the corner and follow its left edge with trees on your left. In about 60 yards, go left over a stile by a 2-way footpath sign. Go ahead passing a pond on the right and continue, climbing gently, to reach a junction by a marker post. Go right descending at first then climbing gradually passing marker posts as you go.

2. Soon you pass through a wooden bridle gate with a National Trust sign for Devil's Dyke in front of you. Keep to the path and climb, steeply in places, to the left of the Dyke. Just keep climbing the path beside the Dyke, taking comfort from the fact that your return journey through the Dyke, after optional refreshments, will be at the bottom so you are getting the hardest bit done now.

As you near the end, look out for the very basic remains of an old cable car system that operated across the valley from 1894-1909. It covered a distance of 350m

Old cable car point over a 100m drop.

and was suspended 70m above the valley floor. As you stand there try to imagine how it would have looked and how popular an attraction it would be if one were built now.

At the end, curve around to the right aiming for a bridle gate in sight with a building behind it. Go through the gate and ahead to a marker post. Go ahead / left uphill to reach the car park via a stile at the Devil's Dyke pub which is very popular especially on a hot day. Before stopping for well-deserved refreshment, go across the road opposite the pub for some lovely views and this area is also popular with kite fliers and paragliders. There is a trig point over to the left and around to the right there is a large stone seat with three information boards showing the local villages and a telescope. From the legend it is these villages that the Devil was trying to flood with sea water when he started the Devil's Dyke.

3. Leave the pub and return through the car park and go back down to the bridle gate. Once through the gate take the obvious path that runs along the bottom of Devil's Dyke; just follow this path appreciating just how high the sides of the Dyke are. (Try to imagine water rushing towards you if the Devil had connected with the sea.)

When you arrive back at the National Trust Devil's Dyke sign do not go back through the bridle gate but instead go left to a stile in view in the field corner. Cross the stile into woodland, go up lots of steps then follow a winding path through the trees, climbing steeply in places. The path soon levels off but then starts to rise gradually again.

At a junction by a marker post, continue ahead by going up six steps and continuing through trees until you reach a swing gate. Do not go through the gate but go right (SLOWLY) down

Paraglider over the Weald villages that the Devil wanted to flood?

loads of steps, over a 100, taking care as they are uneven, steep and can be slippery.

At a marker post with a yellow arrow go right and in a few more yards you reach a junction with another National Trust Devil's Dyke sign. Go left here and follow the wide path down, passing houses to reach a road. Turn right along the road for a few yards to arrive back at the Royal Oak back at the start.

SUGGESTED WALK

WALK 19. Jack and Jill windmills and Clayton Tunnel (4.0 miles 6.4 km)

Parking. There is roadside parking by the Plough pub. (Post code BN45 7FN.) This walk is very hilly going up on to the South Downs Way on the outward journey then over Wolstonbury Hill, which can be very muddy after periods of rain, at the end. There are no stiles. Refreshments are available from the Plough Inn.

1. Facing the Plough pub, walk up Church Lane which is to the right of the pub. At the main road junction, go left along Church Hill and in a few yards, you reach the Church of the Transfiguration. Pay special attention to the Tapsel gate which is unique to this part of Sussex.

(It is a rare design and named after a Sussex family who invented it. Only six remain in the county and all are found within 10 miles of Lewes. This gate is a twentieth century replacement for the original eighteenth century gate and it incorporates the hooked end of a Pyecombe crook – a type of shepherd's staff made in the village since the eighteenth century. The gates are mounted on a central pivot and even when fully open are too narrow to let cattle into the churchyards but they are easier for pallbearers to negotiate than a normal side-hinged gate: they can pass on each side and the coffin can be rested on the central pivot if necessary.)

Return back along Church Hill to the junction and go-ahead down School Lane. At the bottom you reach the busy A273 and just before it you go left by a 3-way footpath sign following the South Downs Way (SDW) with the A273 on your right.

At the end of the path, cross the road and continue up along the SDW into Pyecombe Golf Course directly opposite. You soon reach the golf course car park and on the far side of the car park you follow the enclosed footpath across the golf course following the SDW marker posts and climbing quite steeply with the golf course on either side of you. As you follow the path, near the top of the climb, keep a look out on the left for distant views of the windmills.

Top left: Church of the Transfiguration.

Left: Tapsel gate.

Jill windmill in 2020.

Just keep following the path until you reach a main junction of paths by a 4-way footpath sign. Go left here and continue to follow the SDW, passing farm buildings and enjoying the views as you head towards the windmills. At a 3-way footpath sign continue towards the windmills and soon you reach Jack (black) windmill which compared to Jill does look a bit sorry for itself and tries to hide away behind the trees. Stay on the path and just past Jack you reach a car park on the right; go through the car park with a good view of Jill (white) on the right. These windmills are very well known in Sussex and benefit from the winds blowing in from the English Channel.

St John the Baptist church.

2. On the far side of the car park you reach a bridle gate beside a wide metal gate. Go left here, steeply down across a field never far from the fence on your left and with lovely views all around you. As you descend you are aiming towards the church of St John the Baptist in Clayton which you will soon be walking past.

Soon your path meets with the end of the fence on the left by a 3-way footpath sign. Go left here and follow the chalky path still close to the wire fence and follow it as it curves around to the right aiming for a bridle gate in view by a 4-way footpath sign. Go through the bridle gate and ahead down an uneven path beneath trees.

At the end you reach a lane. Go left along the lane passing St John the Baptist church to reach a main road at the end. If it is open you should go inside the church. It has an extensive set of wall paintings from the early twelfth century that were rediscovered more than 700 years later. Now taking great care, as this can be a very busy junction with cars coming from all directions at speed, cross the main road and turn right with the entrance to Clayton Tunnel on your left. (A good photo is if you can get a train with its lights on as it exits the tunnel.)

3. At the bridge, go left along New Way Lane and in about 130 yards go left along a path as directed by a public bridleway sign. Now follow this path through trees, it can get very muddy and slippery, and climb gradually. Pass a National Trust sign for Wolstonbury Hill and continue to climb steeply to reach a 3-way bridleway sign by a bridle gate where you continue ahead still climbing.

The path levels out by a 4-way footpath sign and a bridle gate on the right. Continue directly ahead with limited distant views of the windmills over to the left. Just follow this path descending to its end then continue ahead along an access road to reach the junction you used on your outward journey. Go ahead, back down Church Lane to reach the Plough for a well-deserved drink.

SUGGESTED WALK

WALK 20. Brighton City Centre (4.0 miles 6.4 km)

Parking. Wherever you want in Brighton. This is a simple, level walk that just takes you around Brighton visiting as many of the main attractions as possible. It is a circular walk so you can start it at whatever point suits you best. This walk is only intended for the handful of people who have never been to Brighton before. I have started it near the West Pier in keeping with the rest of this West Sussex coastal book which travels west to east through the county. There are hundreds of places for refreshments on this walk so don't try to do a pub crawl.

1. From the bandstand/West Pier go along the seafront soon reaching the British Airways i360 viewing tower which in itself is visible from miles around. Continue aiming for the Palace Pier in sight and passing well known hotels such as the Hilton Metropole and the Grand as well as other attractions, shops, bars etc. When you reach the entrance to the Palace Pier a short distance past it on the same side you have the Brighton Zip (a 300m dual zip wire with a 24m drop), crazy golf, and Volks Railway (the oldest electric railway in the world that runs between the Palace Pier and the marina which you can see ahead of you). Almost directly opposite the pier entrance you have the Sea Life centre.

Bandstand and West Pier.

Palace Pier.

2. After visiting the pier, cross the main road by the pedestrian lights to reach the Royal Albion Hotel. Go left along the main road and take the third right up East Street. Go all the way up East Street to its end to reach the entrance to the Royal Pavilion in front of you. Enter the Pavilion grounds and after you have finished return to this entrance.

Crazy golf and Brighton Zip tower.

The Lanes.

3. Return back down East Street and take the first right up North Street. On your way up North Street you will pass a sign for the Lanes on your left if you want to explore them but the walk continues to reach the clock tower at the end of North Street at a junction of roads. Cross the road and go ahead past the clock tower along Western Road opposite. Very soon you reach the entrance to Churchill Square shopping centre on your left if you want to go shopping. The walk continues along Western Road but I always get stopped by the smell of onions at the popular hot dog van and I have to get a burger.

4. After eating your hot dog or burger continue along Western Road, passing more shops as you go. Turn left down Preston Street (it is signed) and at the end you reach the seafront near the West Pier back at the start. I hope this helped a few of you even if it was only for the hot dog. If you can't do it today book a two-night break and come back just to explore the City and you can experience the lively nightlife, bars and restaurants.

Clock Tower.

WEBLIOGRAPHY

www.westsussex.info
www.forces-war-records.co.uk/units/708/raf-thorney-island
www.conservancy.co.uk
www.bosham.org
www.historicengland.org
www.visitsouthernengland.com
www.thebeachguide.co.uk
www.ice.org.uk
www.rspb.org.uk
www.selseylifeboats.co.uk
www.sussextransport.com
www.avonconstruction.com/selsey-bill-tower
www.stpetersselsey.com
www.selseytowncouncil.gov.uk
www.paghamchurch.org
www.chichestercathedral.org
www.thenovium.org
www.chichestercity.gov
www.historicengland.org
www.chichestercanal.org
www.hothampark.co.uk
www.bognorpiertrust.co.uk
www.rampionoffshore.com
www.boxgrovepriory.co.uk
www.english-heritage.org.uk
www.derelictplaces.co.uk
www.wwt.org.uk

www.belloc-broadwood.org.uk/hilaire-belloc-biography
www.middleton-on-sea-pc.gov.uk
www.littlehamptonfort.co.uk
www.coastradar.com
www.bbc.co.uk/news/uk-england-sussex-35595350
www.littlehampton.org.uk
www.eastbeachcafe.co.uk
www.rustingtonvillage.co.uk/history
www.motorsportmagazine.com/archive/article/april-1983/78/air-speed-record
www.ferringhistorygroup.co.uk
www.stmarysbramber.co.uk
www.explorechurches.org/church/st-nicholas-bramber
www.lancingcollege.co.uk
www.yee.co.uk/adur-ferry-bridge-west-sussex
www.scottishpower.com/userfiles/file/Shoreham-Site-Information-2014.pdf
www.adur-worthing.gov.uk/seafront-and-river-adur/rnli-coastguard-and-lighthouse
www.Shoreham-port.co.uk/Wind-Energy/southwick
www.southwicksociety.btck.co.uk/SouthwickRomanVilla
www.arthurlloyd.co.uk/Brighton/WestPier.htm
https://mybrightonandhove.org.uk/places/placesea/seafront-attractions
www.visitsoutheastengland.com/places-to-visit/sussex/map

ADDITIONAL SOURCES OF INFORMATION

Information boards at numerous attractions and places of interest.

Novium Museum Chichester

Domesday Book – Penguin Classics 'A Complete Translation' ISBN 0-141-43994-7

All photos taken by Phil Christian

SELECTIVE INDEX